湖南省社科基金外语科研联合项目成果（21WLH12）
湖南省教育厅科学研究重点项目成果（22A0229）
本书获长沙理工大学学术出版资助

Study on Language Redundancy and Its Functions

语言中的冗余及其功能探析

阎 瑾◎著

湘潭大学出版社

图书在版编目（CIP）数据

语言中的冗余及其功能探析 / 阎瑾著. -- 湘潭 :
湘潭大学出版社, 2022.12
ISBN 978-7-5687-1022-0

Ⅰ. ①语… Ⅱ. ①阎… Ⅲ. ①语言学一研究 Ⅳ.
① H0

中国国家版本馆 CIP 数据核字 (2023) 第 034674 号

语言中的冗余及其功能探析

YUYAN ZHONG DE RONGYU JIQI GONGNENG TANXI

阎瑾 著

责任编辑：姚海琼
封面设计：于 扬
出版发行：湘潭大学出版社
社 址：湖南省湘潭大学工程训练大楼
电 话：0731-58298960 0731-58298966（传真）
邮 编：411105
网 址：http://press.xtu.edu.cn/
印 刷：长沙创峰印务有限公司
经 销：湖南省新华书店
开 本：710 mm×1000 mm 1/16
印 张：11.25
字 数：203 千字
版 次：2022年12月第1版
印 次：2023年1月第1次印刷
书 号：ISBN 978-7-5687-1022-0
定 价：45.00 元

前 言

冗余现象是广泛存在于各种语言的现象。它存在于语言的各个层面,如语音、句法、语义层面等。冗余是语言作为一种交际工具的固有特征。它是自然的口头语言和文字语言中包含的多余的语言和非语言信息,即不属于理解语言必不可少的信息。冗余信息是语言交际过程中信息差的表现之一,它同语言的经济原则相对立,同时又会反作用于正常的信息传输,造成信息损耗,降低语言的使用效率。然而,从语义内容与语言发展的规律来看,冗余现象的产生又是不可避免的。在实际的言语交际中,言语表达并不是越简洁越好,言语表达中处处充满着冗余。事实上,语言冗余现象存在于各种语言之中、各种语体之中,成为言语交际必不可少的重要手段。

冗余之所以成为一种客观存在的语言事实,定有其存在的合理性和必然性。基于前人的研究和对相关语料的分析,本书重点就这种语言现象从语用的角度展开讨论,证实其存在的价值,并尝试性地探讨其存在的隐性动因,以求进一步认识和了解冗余的本质和功能。"冗余"这个概念源于信息科学并被借用到其它很多领域,为了避免混淆,本书首先对冗余的概念作了一个界定。在对以往的冗余定义进行概括分析之后,本书指出了各定义的优点和存在的不足,总结出冗余的基本特征,从而依此提出冗余的工作定义。这里我们将其理解为在特定语境中任何可以取消或简化的语言单位,即如果一个语言单位所传达的信息已经蕴含在其它语言单位,或者这种语言信息可以用更简洁的方式表达或与要表达的用意无关,那么这个语言单位便是冗余信息。根据此定义,本书将各种冗余表现形式概括为结构上的冗余和意义上的冗余两大类,前者包括重复和话语标记语,后者包括迂说和蕴含。界定了冗余之后,本书重点从会话含义和语篇两个方面对其进行了解释和分析。一方面,鉴于冗余的一个重要语用功能是产生会话含义,本书借助语用学中关于会话含义的有代表性的理论来理解和解释冗余并利用语料对其各种表现形式进行了详细的分析。另一方面,本书从语篇的角度,采用典型的语料探讨了冗余在语篇中的修辞效果和语篇功能。其修辞效果主要包括冗余在语篇中所起的强调、表达和描写方面的作用。语篇功能则主要体现在冗余能使口头和书面表达更具有整体性和连贯性。通过在上述两个方面的讨论,从语用的视角证实了语言冗余现象存在的价值。在此基础上本书认为,冗余既然作为一种有价值的语言现象而普遍存在,其存在肯定具有其必然性。在此基础上,本书进而探讨了冗余存在的隐性动因,其主要包括目的驱使、心理需求、文体需要、文化影响和性别差异这五个方面的因素。探讨这些使之合理存在的原因,将有助于我们对冗余这种语言现象在本质上有进一步的了解。

语言冗余现象的研究对解释各种语言现象、对语言教学、翻译、影视和文学鉴赏等具有重要的指导意义。同时,研究冗余的意义不仅仅在于语言学本身,更对其他学科,如社会语言学、认知心理学、脑神经科学、社会文化学的发展具有深刻的启示。在人类社会迈向全球化信息时代、我国步入互联网大国行列的时代背景下,研究语言的理解和使用的学问显得尤为重要。我们应当客观、科学地对待语言中的冗余现象。

目 录

CONTENTS

Preface

Before starting the discussion in this book, I must remind my readers of a story titled "the blind men and an elephant" which originated in the Indian subcontinent from where it has widely diffused. The most common version of the story is about several blind men who touch an elephant to learn what it is like. Lack of their ocular inspection, each man felt the elephant with his palm in the darkness. One touched the trunk and said that the elephant was like a water-spout. The hand of another happened to lay on the elephant's ear and he thought the beast was apparently like a huge fan. Another announced the shape of the elephant was like a column by rubbing against its leg. Another felt the belly of the elephant and had an impression that the beast was like a wall. The last two who touched the tusk and the tail of that elephant drew conclusions respectively that the animal was either like a spear or like a rope. The man who could see the elephant finally said: "You are all partially correct. The Elephant has features that you explained but it is much more". In Sufi Poet and Mystic Rumi's words, the moral of the story is: The sensual eye is just like the palm of the hand. The palm has not the means of covering the whole of the beast.

However, we know the world surrounding us not only by our palms and eyes, but also by something else. Language, the miraculous gift from somewhere we are not so sure, helps us separate ourselves from other species. Without language, we human beings cannot announce us as the master of the world and it is not exaggerated to say that language, more than anything else, creates us. Nobody can deny the fact that our infinite thoughts expressed and shared by the unique power of language are crucial to all humans societies, and definitely language, such a gift granted to human, has played a key role in the rise of our species on the past three million years from a weak and obscure group of the east African continent to the dominant species on the earth today. In spite of constant searching and researching, it seems that nowhere in the planet can we discover any communication system enjoying equivalent power as our language, neither in animal kingdom nor in plant world. In the last two to three million years, our human language has undergone a long process of evolution which is undoubtedly one of the most significant and arresting events during the history of our earth. Considering its core role in humans culture and behavior, it is not surprising that the origin of language has been a topic of myth, legend and speculation ever before the starting of history. When modern Darwinian evolutionary theory has been established and exerts its influence on all species on the earth, more and more people cannot help asking questions about the evolution of language, and these questions have avoidably accelerated a rapid trend of the growth of scientific literature. Since the later decades of last century, scholars with various backgrounds such as linguistics, oratory, anthropology, sociology, neuroscience, psychology and evolutionary biology keep on devoting themselves to probing into different aspects of the evolution of language. The result of such enthusiasm means a vast scientific and technical literature extending across a great number of subjects or fields, and much of it aimed at audiences with special training and knowledge. Nevertheless, the purpose of the following chapter is to survey the related data and achievements of language from a comparatively object viewpoint. In my opinion, the most significant issue annoying this realm is vividly represented by the parable of the elephant told at the beginning of this book.

Frankly, language is so complicated and central to humans that it penetrates all perspectives of human's behavior, culture, society and cognition. Researchers of many different subjects can fairly assert their insights into its workings. After more than ten years of language learning, teaching and studying, I affirm that many researchers have surely gained insights into our language, and of course some of them are quite far-reaching. However, because the language system is so complicated that there is no one researcher or subject has yet achieved an sufficiently comprehensive overview. Like those blind men in that elephant parable touching the beast in the darkness, all of us are painstakingly exploring the language in the darkness and all of us can partially understand language and each subject will have its position in the profound description and understanding that all are seeking.

It can be imagined that the diversity of different aspects can be confusing. For example, in the aspect of linguistics, Noam Chomsky puts his emphasis on syntax and he points out that the biology of language is composed of a highly abstract core of syntax. In the aspect of psychology, two psychologists with high reputation, Michael Tomasello and Ellen Markman, show different interests in language. The former notices that the existence of language has much to do with the humans capability for the shared purposes, while the latter insists that language acquisition has a very close relationship with a suite of detailed constraints which carries a certain possible meaning. Philip Lieberman, a cognitive scientist, studies language from the angle of speech science and proves that the motor control is crucial to our language. Luc Steels, however, through his research realm of computer science, expects that the meaning of language comes from a social, perceiving and motivational foundation with a broad sense. When his colleagues in the field of neuroscience think that language is in the mirror neurons shared by us with primates, Terrence Deacon fixes his eyes on the neural foundation for our thought in symbolic sense in the highly-evolved prefrontal cortex of mankind. Undoubtedly, protolanguage should appear in a certain period of our humans language and there should be a kind of intermediate stage such as protolanguage. Derek Bickerton assumes linguistically that this system includes words of individuals, much the same as those used by children less than two years old. Gordon Hewes asserts anthropologically that the face and hands can gesturally convey the information of protolanguage, while Charles Darwin tried to convince us of the fact that this kind of language was expressed in the way of song—like phrases. Besides the above mentioned opinions, someone refers to the connection of sound and meaning as a whole, while others take it as a system unavoidably inconsistent and compositional. Someone pays attention to the inner pressures which makes language adaptive, and someone takes heed of the so-called ordinary natural choice, and someone adheres to the gender's selection. As far as I am concerned, family members' choices play a very important role in the language's evolution. As far as for the language's function in the communication for the purpose information exchange's is concerned, or the language's role in building our human's thought, scholars seem evenly divided in their personal major or aspect. Nevertheless, when some researchers think that the leaps in evolution play a particularly significant role, emphasizing the discontinuities and disconnections between language and in other animals, some others insist that gradual change and evolutionary continuity between humans and other species should be the perspective which we put stress on. All these issues have been painstakingly studied and discussed for years. However, it seems that a final resolution is hardly achieved. The purpose of writing this book and the key argument in it is to acknowledge the weaknesses and advantages of each researcher's opinion and then try to converge and integrate all these mechanisms, which will represent one facet of language and the characteristics of language. By means of this, I not only wants to tell the readers that language enjoys a salient feature of division and unproductivity. Here I want to remind the readers of the parable cited at the beginning of the book, from which we can understand how important it is for us to make a reconciliation among contradictory ideas and aspects. Honestly, a sufficient knowledge of the evolution of language demand us to do it, to reconcile many opposite ideas mentioned above.

Frankly, the core discussion of this book is that language, after so many years evolution, is often taken granted by people that any unnecessary words or phrases can only do harm for our daily expression. Almost everyone wants to use the simplest way to talk and write, not only for energy saving, but also for the favor of their listeners. Without any doubt, one will feel embarrassed if others think that his talking or writing is "wordy" "verbose" or "awkward". Conversely, "as brief as the Bible" "simplicity" "concise" and "succinct" are popular praises for those who are good at expression and of course these kinds of phrases and words are what people would like to hear. Nevertheless, an evolution over so many years can make language so complicated that each of the scholars listed above has mastered some true and reliable opinion about language, but none of these opinions are complete in themselves. I insist that language requires the combination and convergence of diverse mechanisms, and every one of them is indispensible but no one alone is adequate. In order to prove that "redundancy" of language is necessary and some seemingly redundant words, phrases even sentences can really play a positive role in our expression, arguments about the evolution of language, difference of the formation of language and each core opinion of the feature of language are avoidable for these can help my readers to understand more of my study on the functions of "language redundancy". Just as the parable I have cited above, it pushes us to make an obvious reconciliation of contradictory perspective. I affirmatively hold an idea that a broad and complete understanding of the evolution of language demands us to reconcile many of the opposite ideas mentioned above.

In fact, a very popular variant of the elephant parable lets us know that a group of blind scholars are called by a king to study the elephant, and a fight breaks out because they persist in an opinion that what they "see" and their interpretations are quite different. I do not like this kind of version and I insist that the version I have selected is better, considering that in terms of language, actually there is no such a brightly-sighted king who can own a panoramic view of that entire beast and all of us have only partial insights and we can only see an iceberg above water.

Sad to say, the belligerent conclusion of the variant of the elephant parable often applies to study on language evolution, since the argument and dispute on language have been witnessed everywhere. In the past decades, I have frequently seen a lot of respected scholars and researchers criticizing each other for the ignorance of language, the ignorance of the evolution of humans brain, or other relevant topics. For researchers, whenever they feel that they can take the upper wind during the dispute, they will reproach others' negligence of a certain point or failure of understanding the essence of language.

Needless to say, nobody, as I myself cannot be an exception, has an comprehensive overview of language evolution, therefore, the purpose of writing this book is not to give the answers or resolve all debates among the circle of intelligent. Rather, it will proffer an overview of the functions of language redundancy based on the full-scale understanding of language, the various types of information of the debates. I will try to accept each useful and necessary integration of the synthesis. Some of the data can self-evidently help us to resolve the issues of dispute for years in language evolution and these issues stem from those different disciplines, say, from linguistics to molecular biology, from sociology to anthropology, from history to psychology. Certainly, none can brag that he can have the ability to master all the discipline above. Thus, we can indicate that scholars must make cooperation with each other to achieve broader and more convincing results. Surely, answers to the tough questions about a huge topic as language evolution, which of course contains some most profound and meaningful questions about humans nature, require cooperation and teamwork among different disciplines of a sort that is quite rare in the present field. My central and simple purpose in this book's writing is not only to enhance the potential cooperation by offering a certain access to the insights from many related fields to readers who are interested in them, but also present the topic of redundancy, which is often neglected by us, to those who want to know more of the miracle befell on our humans beings, hoping to stimulate more people's enthusiasm in language phenomenon.

The Essence of This book

This book, based on a full-scale introduction of the interdisciplinary study of language evolution, emphasizing the necessity and importance of the combination of various disciplines, such as the theory of evolution, the theory of archaeology, paleoanthropology, humans genetics, historical comparative linguistics, comparative linguistics and cognitive linguistics. Traditionally, biology and linguistics seldom move forward hand in hand, but there is a growing tendency that a discipline is combined in the formation of the so-called bio-linguistics. Indebt to this promising combination, or even synthesis, the topic of language evolution becomes more interesting and productive. Although I cannot say that the book fills the gap in language study, I still think that this book can provide readers with a new and broad way to know more about the secret and charm of language, because few people, at least in China at present, attempt to offer a comprehensive overview of this sort of information. Instead, most of the books, favoring a peculiar hypothesis or point of view, will offer long and detailed disputes based on the author's personal interest. In my opinion, the field is ready for an objective survey of the available hypotheses and an assessment of their strengths and weaknesses according to the current data available. Since the book is problem-oriented, it will try to utilize the hypothesis-testing stance of the achievements of different disciplines. For the essence of this book, how to use these results and how to combine them with each other will be the main concern, because these can help me get rid of the obstacles in my study on the topic of "language redundancy". In spite of the fact that I have my own perspective on these problems and my own ideas about the certain hypotheses, I am eager to arouse the readers' interest and I really hope that the readers can have their own conclusion by offering them an overview of the relevant questions, approaches and statistics without any prejudice. In order to keep the balance, I will try to remain an objective attitude when I deal with the information available.

A Polyphyletic and Multivariant Perspective

Basically, the central hypothesis of my method is that we should refer language as a system combining variant factors, which means it is composed of different components, partially separated. It is well known that other animals also share some of these components. For example, the ability of listening, remembering and cognizing and vocalizing. However, it must be noticed that humans are distinguished from chimpanzee, orangutan or gorilla by only a few components, such as the ability of vocal acquisition and using complicated sentences. These primates are definitely regarded as our closest relatives. Essentially and noticeably, these indispensable components of language may convincingly enjoy their own history of evolution and they depend upon divided mechanisms of the nerve system and gene structure. Language, of course, is a delicate system characterized by mutual effect and interplay of these multiple components, without any gap or seam among them, but language is by no means a monolithic whole.

Although language is a system characterized by seamless interaction among these multiple components, "language" is by no means a lonely existence, and from a biological perspective, we would see it as a sack of a magician, which is accumulated piece by piece through a long period of evolution. To a certain extent, this perspective about the multi-component structure is not incorrect. Therefore, I dare to say that any attempt to choose an aspect of language as a core or centre is either excessive subjective or incorrect. Next, I want my readers to know that the second central part of my method comes from this opinion: statistics from a broad series of animals to check and prove theories of language evolution are what I rely upon. In fact, some unknown species can also own some components of our language. For example, the ability of acquisitioning complicated sound, which is owned by some birds, dolphins and seals, can promise our children to learn words or phrases from a certain language shared by their neighbors in the same community. However, it is quite curious that this kind of ability is not shared by any other primate, no matter how clever they are. Making an investigation of such features requires a very extensively comparative method, including a wide array of species. Thus, the readers will find out that either detailed study of chimpanzee and other primates, or birds, dolphin, seals and even deer will be mentioned in this book. There is no doubt that an exclusive focus on our closest relatives, primates actually, will misguide readers of this book, and neglecting many other species with lessons to let us know more about our language will bring us a great many of risks. Nevertheless, I am willing to accept the point that our humans language is definitely unique. In spite of the fact that language in its pure humans form is still unique to ourselves, it depends upon a wide series of biological mechanisms shared by other species. Our incomparable gift—language promises us to express what we are thinking and convey our thoughts through a sort of mutually understandable signals. Here I do not say that animals do not communicate because so many documentaries and books tell us that animals definitely communicate for survival. However, the communication of all animals is not the same with ours and ours is a must which singles humans out from other species. Surely enough, human, alone in our earth, is the only species having this particular ability. This fact is of no more surprise to evolutionary biologists than other unusual characteristics like pigeon's location, elephant's trunk or vertical landing of honeybee. Apparently, these cited examples tell us all these unique features share components with other organisms, and in this way language is of no exception. Taking study on communication and cognition of animals at present, we can easily see that some aspects of language are unique to our humans for sure. It is quite possible that each component or subcomponent of language is shared by one species or another. Fortunately, only we humans can put them together seamlessly. In other words, although most components are commonly shared by other species, a few of them in our humans language capability are still unique to us. These questions are empirical and solving them demands us to take a close look at the similarities and differences between humans language and animal communication and cognition. Finally, the principle which helps me to write this book is my optimistic attitude and mentality to try to analyze many disputes available. Truly speaking, my optimism is directly against the well-known idea that there are no statistics related to the evolution of language. It is obvious that we have no time machine to go back to the time that we cannot experience at present, so we say our language is alive. Its uncertainty, however, does not mean that the study of language is out of the range of science and violate the law of science. Supposing that we do not have any video records of our ancestor's oral expression, or we do not have any historically grounded science from geology to paleontology, we cannot do any research of what we are interested in. Invariably, we need to use many indirect evidences in all these fields and statistics available to set scientific constraints upon attempts at language evolution modeling. What is more, powerful searching engine and the data online today can give us more opportunities to test hypotheses about the biology and the evolution of language. Taking two as examples, we can see that modern non-invasive brain imaging can give us chance to check models of cognitive "modules" and to test relationships among those models. By means of this, the fact that the hypothesis of Darwin's protolanguage is correlatively connected with such data is quite direct. And much the same, molecular genetic techniques, which is partially applied to modern humans today, expose us to the chance of the estimation about the times at which genes involved in our speech populated among our ancestors long gone. At last, as more and more genetic achievements for language are accumulated, we are lucky to have this method to guarantee us to decide the order in which various components of language evolved in our humans. In any case, the appearance of these new kinds of techniques unfolds us an exciting prospect. It can be imagined that disputes concerning language evolution, which have been lasting for decades, will resolve some problems that we are facing up with. Although my review will definitely be casted to a substantial amount of factual knowledge, I must point out that the book is either open-question-oriented or answer-oriented. Actually, my purpose and goal of writing this book is to offer the readers a chance to come closer to some theoretical tools and factual database to understand those questions. At the same time, I also want to provide the readers with an invitation to take part in the broad, cooperative interdisciplinary exchange which is of great necessity for our future study. In my deep heart, I wish that the readers can partly get rid of the influence of previous information or data and become proficient on several different perspectives and hypotheses of language evolution. In this way, they will have a strong desire to add some new statistics and test the accuracy of them in time. If so, the data will be accessible and it will help us to observe the perspective of language acquisition, or help us to notice some unusual sentence structures online when we are surfing on the Internet. Even we can envision that many proposals and projects in language learning will be granted greatly, which will bring about a glorious future of English learning and teaching in China. I would humbly believe myself to be successful if this book could inspire a great many researchers to fix their eyes on such new questions and eventually give us at least a few valuable answers.

Structure of the Book

The first chapter of this book is a an introduction and a review, which is by and large a survey of humans history of evolution, theories of evolution, cognition and communication of animals, and humans language researches. Through the process of giving the readers an introduction to the main issues and hypotheses, references of necessary background material and statistics will come, which means that I plan to present a comparative and comprehensive overviews of the disciplines and data involved in an quickly growing field. Of course, I cannot avoid some jargons but I will try to use plain and understandable way to let my readers to catch them easily. Despite that fact that I cannot justify many academic disciplines in this book, I still hope that the first chapter can enable the readers to move further and explore more, and finally to assess the models of language evolution at present by themselves. The content of the first chapter will involve the solution to the question that there are no data related to the evolution of language, and at the first glance this seems indirect or irrelevant though, all of the data will be brought to use more or less later in this book. The beginning of a survey of evolutionary theory will give us a summary of those fundamental principles applied to the research of contemporary biology, helping estimate the possibility and validity of those hypotheses of evolution. It cannot be denied that during the long process of language evolution, some unique problems unavoidably appear. This phenomenon is normal and may demand something new to be added to contemporary evolutionary theory, but this issue should not be biased by us. Instead, we should use our logic and try to make it evolutionarily standard in many organisms and features. It seems that some theorists hold the belief that the evolution of language breaks the law of evolution, however, I will point out that this intuition may be wrong and that contemporary theory of evolution has already possessed certain resources of conception to deal with, and in fact it brings strong restraint to theories of language evolution. After my discussion of the evolutionary theory, I think the readers will have an overview of language, the miracle that we humans have luckily obtained for so many years.

Next, based on the first Chapter, I will move on to the topic of an interesting aspect of language-redundancy. By a brief demonstration of the existence of this peculiar trait of language, I will provide the readers a literature review, citing various studies and achievements in this special field. Many foreign studies will be my concern because in this field, westerners, frankly speaking, have done much ahead and with systematical and theoretical insights. Nonetheless, as a Chinese researcher, I will undoubtedly pay more attention to the achievements in China in the past twenty years. The reason why I will do this is that traditionally our Chinese have a special complex in the preference of a simple and concise language, both in oral and written ways. Furthermore, in the past three decades, scholars, especially scholars in language teaching, have noticed the importance of various obstacles in foreign language teaching and learning. In China, ESL is by all means the biggest concern for educators, and the whole country has invested a lot in it. When redundancy is literally mentioned, it means some language components are superfluous and useless. But after reading the researches over these years, contrary to what should be, scholars in China strongly feel that redundancy plays an important role in the acceptance of information for language, and redundancy itself is a kind of content and it certainly carries a bundle of meanings. Thus, redundancy contributes to the processing of meaning and for most of the time plays an active part whether in written forms or in oral forms. Many scholars are intended to find out some rules by analyzing different examples taken from different resources. Although some think that redundancy has negative effect on our discourse, some insist that redundancy can do more good than harm. No matter how uncompromised they are, they cannot deny the existence of redundancy in our language. Truly speaking, the debate among these scholars can enlarge our horizon and help us to notice redundancy, a common phenomenon but always overlooked by people. According to Information Theory, redundancy is counted as a means of overcoming noise. Nida, a famous American scholar, believes that redundancy reflects predictability in language. Chinese scholar Qian Guanlian thinks that the use of redundancy is motivated by communication goals and that the use of appropriate redundancy can help achieve communicative goals. Wang Hong classifies redundancy into repetition, circumlocution, verbal fillers and phatic communion. To the same topic of redundancy, Chinese scholars, such as Xu Shenghuan, Gui Shichun and the like, also express their ideas and even cite a lot of examples literally and practically. We hold that redundancy is a way to achieve certain communicative effects, and appropriate redundancy can play a positive role in language practice and employment.

Chapter Three, after synthesizing the previous achievements of scholars at home and abroad, tries to provide a working definition of redundancy. Its purpose is quite obvious, that is, in order to help the readers to understand more of the latter chapter, I attempt to employ a full-scale viewpoint and work out a reasonable definition of redundancy. Without any doubt, different researchers hold their different views on the term "redundancy". Some of them express their ideas from the aspect of translation, some of them give their assertions from the perspective of rhetoric, and some of them fix their eyes on ESL. Anyway, a working definition can help others to understand their opinion more, and of course my working definition is to convince the readers of my analysis. Chapter Four, essentially, is a firm foundation of chapter five and chapter six, which expound some positive functions of redundancy from pragmatic aspects because essentially redundancy has much to do with the daily use of language. Pragmatically, redundancy is indispensably correlated with the Cooperative Principle, politeness and Speech Act Theory, etc,. Proper use of redundancy can help observe Cooperative Principle on one hand, and flout Cooperative Principle for specialimplication on the other hand. In addition, redundancy contributes to politeness in language and it can even create a sense of beauty in language expression. It must be pointed out that redundancy is also often used in indirect speech acts. What is more, redundancy can produce humorous effects, remove ambiguity of a sentence and perform phatic function. Rhetorically, repetition, a kind of redundancy as well as a kind of figure of speech, is widely used in literary works to achieve different effects. And in this chapter, several types of repetition and their functions will be discussed. Via a lot of live examples taken from various resources, this chapter will offer the readers a better vision of redundancy. Thereby, a sensible understanding of redundancy can be achieved consequently.

Chapter Five is mainly concerned with redundancy in text. A lot of samples will be cited from different resources, such as *Vanity Fair*, plays of William Shakespeare and even daily conversations. It is obvious that redundancy, when used, can achieve various effects, like emphatic effect, expressive effect and descriptive effect, as well as unity and cohesion in textual function. In this chapter, how to analyze those samples is of great difficulty because what I am worried about is the subjectivity, which sometimes will certainly influence the researcher's judgment. However, in the light of redundancy's effect and function, what I have analyzed can be useful, at a certain degree, for language learning. In terms of language employment, speakers and writers, from their point of view, will consciously or unconsciously take what they want to express to achieve a certain pragmatic purpose into consideration.

Chapter Six is devoted to an in-depth analysis of the factor that may affect the degree of redundancy. Firstly, I want to point out that motivation will play a vital role in the appearance of redundancy. Just as humans' other behaviors, language is an externalization of thoughts. Most of our language is produced and expressed with certain purpose. Secondly, context as another factor will influence the degree of redundancy. Since we do not repeat information which has already existed in context, context has a screening function on information. Thirdly, different functions that language performs will lead to different degree of redundancy, as we can see in the samples from the former chapter. The forth factor is style. The more formal the style is, the more redundant the language will be. Moreover, some cultural, social and even gender factors can also affect the degree of redundancy.

A conclusion is drawn at the end of this book. I wish to assume that the use of redundancy is a kind of linguistic choice and even a subconscious alternative by speaker who is willing to make successful communication for his or her special purpose. And the only concern for redundancy is the degree of its use. Abusing it will arouse the listener's misunderstanding or even aversion, while appropriate employment of redundancy is a communicative necessity and it can achieve certain effect which cannot be done via simplicity or conciseness in our language use.

序言部分提出了本书的研究问题和研究背景,当从字面上提到冗余时,它意味着一些语言成分是多余的和无用的。但是冗余在语言接受信息的过程中起着重要的作用,并且冗余本身也是一种内容,它承载着一系列的意义。因此,冗余有助于意义的处理,无论是书面形式还是口头形式,在大多数时候都起着积极的作用。本部分还介绍了研究设计、方法和本书的结构安排。

Chapter 1 Language Evolution: Disciplines and Data

Real evidence is what modern science usually and essentially puts stress on. Crucially, many Hominids fossils' excavation all over the world guarantees a big progress about the origin and evolution of humans beings. Although there exist different ideas in some fossils' definition and interpretation, and even some heated arguments about the origin of modern human, facing those fossils, anyone, unless he or she does not respect science, will acknowledge a basic evolution process: humans comes from ancient anthropoid. By contrast, yet there is no remarkable breakthrough in the research of language origin. Objectively speaking, it is difficult for researchers to seek out evidence for the in-depth study.

Language initially is an oral behavior or oral behavior with gestures or kinesics. Unfortunately, this kind of behavior cannot leave us any tracks because of a self-evident problem, that is, no technique records it. The earliest trace of humans language left by ancient humans is character. Nevertheless, even the earliest characters, for example, cuneiform (popular in ancient Near East) and hieroglyph (widely used in ancient Egypt), have only a short history of around five to six thousand years. However, more than fifty thousand years ago, oral language of humans definitely existed. Therefore, the record of character can provide us with evidence about a certain language or the evolution of a certain language family, but it cannot prove the origin of humans language. In addition, because of the continuity of language, that is to say, the language used by previous generation and younger generation should be basically identical, the language used by ancient people can be traced more or less in modern language. Since the 18 th century, historical comparative linguists have been trying to propose various protolanguages. However, it is acknowledged that historical comparative method can only propose protolanguage used no more than ten thousand years ago. As for the situation ahead of the history, experts will be quite embarrassed because they have nothing to say. Due to the lack of evidence, different hypotheses appeared long before, including bow-bow theory, the pooh-pooh theory, the yo-heave-ho theory, and the la-la theory of Otto Jespersen, sound sensible at a certain degree, but in fact these hypotheses are essentially speculation or surmise.

Recently, some new theories have been brought up by scholars. For instance, the "grooming theory" mentioned by Aitchison (2000) assumes that ancient humans replace the primate's grooming behavior by gossiping, and by means of this they maintain the relationship among them. Besides, another theory titled as the "deceiving theory" indicates that the behavior of cheating bringing the growth of thecranial capacity and intelligence results in the possibility of language's establishment. Some scholars, such as Hewes (1972), Kimura (1976), Lyons (1988) and Armstrong (1995) and the like, after seeing that higher primates like chimpanzees can have a certain series of signed language despite the absence of vocal language, picked out the "gesture theory" of the 18 th century and re-confirmed that the origin of language is from gesture. Similarly, these new theories or renovated theories are said to have certain sense, however, they still have the same problem: lack of evidence.

It seems that the issue of language origin is something that can never be proved and there is no hope to have a final conclusion. What we may prove is a rough period and the place of language origin. In the past 30 years, all researches and related achievements have been done from these two aspects. In terms of discipline, scholars are ranged from different fields as paleoanthropology, archeology, primatology and linguistics. All in all, the evidence they have brought about is various. Although the evidence is indirect, it is a great progress that some is better than none. As the evidence used by scholars is various, their opinions of the origin of language are consequently different. Furthermore, even in a discipline various opinions still exist. Therefore, the study on language origin presents itself with a situation that different thoughts co-exist.

In her book, Aitchison pointed out that the earliest time of the origin of humans language "can be traced back to two hundred and fifty thousand years ago, or averagely language originated one hundred thousand years ago, or at least fifty thousand years ago" (2000). She presumed that language which appeared two hundred and fifty thousand years ago is kind of simple language (2000). However, later on she quoted the idea of Deacon (1992) by saying that "the cranial capacity of humans and humans language grow together". According to the latter opinion, the time of the appearance of humans language may be much earlier, say, around the time of Homo habilis, which was more than two million years ago. The reason is simple because the cranial capacity of Homo habilis is bigger than that of Australopithecines. The speculations about the ideas of "more than two million years ago" "two hundred and fifty thousand years ago" "one hundred thousand years ago", or "fifty thousand years ago" are not surprising. Anyway, these various ideas present different conclusions from different scholars in different disciplines.

1.1 Evolution of Brain, Vocal Tract and Origin of Language

In the recent decades, one of the most important disciplines pushing the research of language origin forward is paleoanthropology. It is because of the peculiarity of humans communication that the origin and evolution of humans language will be involved into the research of the origin and evolution of human. It is well known that our language is constrained by three biological factors: the input system (mainly sense of hearing and sense of vision, especially the latter); central nerve system and output system (mainly the organ of voicing). It seems that the research of ancient human's sense of hearing and vision does not have much achievement because of the following two reasons. This first one is that, human's sense of hearing and vision are no advanced than those of higher primates. They are finalized and very sophisticated. In the past millions of years, they have not been changed much. Therefore, it is unnecessary for us to do much research on them. The second one is that, organs of hearing and vision are soft tissues and it is impossible for them to be kept as fossils. Paleoanthropologists cannot do anything about it even they really want to probe into them. Consequently, the main focus of their research on language origin is usually on the relationship among the evolution of human's brain, vocal tract organs and the language origin. The most reliable evidence of paleoanthropologists is human's skull fossil.

As for the issue of the time of language origin, there exists inconsistency between paleoanthropologists whose research focus is hominid's nerve system (mainly brain) and organs of voicing (mainly the structure of vocal tract) respectively. Some of the former group insist that origin and evolution of language, origin of humans and evolution of humans brain should occur at the same time. Some paleoanthropologists as Deacon (1992), Leakey (1994), Wilkins and Wakefield (1995) believed that more than two million years ago Homo habilis started to use primal language. Some others as Holloway (1976, 1983) and Falk (1980) inferred that the system of humans language may be traced back to an ancient time, more than three million years ago when Australopithecus began to have their communicative system. They asserted that the system of humans language should be an extension and a development of primate's calling-responding system.

At first, we need to exclude the communicative system from our language. Although Australopithecus is categorized as Hominids, it does not mean that they are humans already. Professor Raymond Dart, the first person who recognized the fossils of Hominids, did not name that humans ancestor as Homo, but called it as Australopithecus africanus instead. This kind of Homo animal usually walks upright. From this point it is human's ancestor indeed, but it is generally closer to ape. Later, more and more fossils of Hominids were discovered constantly. Among these fossils, there are the ones of Australopithecus afarensis (three million and two hundred thousand years ago), represented by that famous Lucy[1]; the ones of Ardipithecus ramidus (around four million and four hundred thousand years ago); the ones of Ardipithecus ramidus Kadabba (around five million and fifty thousand years ago); the ones of Australopithecus robustus and Australopithecus robustus boisei (around one million and eighty hundred years ago). All these ancient apes are categorized into Homo because of the upright way they walk. However, in other aspects, especially in the aspect of cranial capacity, they are of no difference from other apes. As a consequence, they are all named after terms as "-pithecus". Since the last two decades of the 20 th century, the common view achieved by most paleoanthropologists has been that Australopithecus afarensis is closer to apes instead of humans (for details see Pilbeam, 1988). Accordingly, the calling-responding system of Australopithecus afarensis should be closer to that of other kinds of ancient apes.

Around two million and two million five hundred thousand years ago, through the evolution one branch of Australopithecus afarensis came closer to humans. The carnal capacity of this kind of ancient ape has increased by about 50%, reaching 600 cm^3 – 800 cm^3. At the same time, they mastered a skill of making simple stone tools. Therefore, paleoanthropologists think that this kind of ancient ape has broken away from ape and formally became an early member of human. In consideration of tool-making, paleoanthropologists

[1] Lucy is the common name of AL 288-1, several hundred pieces of bone fossils representing 40 percent of the skeleton of a female of the hominin species Australopithecus afarensis. In Ethiopia, the assembly is also known as Dinkinesh, which means "you are marvelous" in the Amharic language. Lucy was discovered in 1974 near the village Hadar in the Awash Valley of the Afar Triangle in Ethiopia by paleoanthropologist Donald Johanson. Lucy acquired her name from the song "Lucy in the Sky with Diamonds" by the Beatles, which was played loudly and repeatedly in the expedition camp all evening after the excavation team ' s first day of work on the recovery site. After public announcement of the discovery, Lucy captured much public interest, becoming almost a household name at the time.

naturally refer to this kind of ape as "Homo habilis". It is reasonable to say that the communicative system of Australopithecus afarensis should be human's language, since this kind of ancient ape is categorized into humans race. Anthropologist Falk (1989) has ever asked: "If Homo is not using and perfecting language, so what they are doing by using their augmenting brain which is autocatalytic?"① However, the question is not so simple. As a matter of fact, the reason that anthropologist named those ancient ape as "Homo habilis" is that they have more characteristics which is closer to human, compared with Australopithecus afarensis. Thus, it is not suitable for anthropologists to name them with "-pithecus". Nonetheless, if we compare them with modern human, we can easily tell the differences between the two groups. According to the estimation of a famous anthropologist, Johanson (1996), the carnal capacity of early Homo habilis is only half of that of humans today, and the percentage of upper limbs and lower limbs between the former and the latter is 95 to 100. From this data, we can say that Homo habilis is theoretically close to chimpanzee. The adult female of Homo habilis is about one meter tall, almost the same as the height of Lucy, representative of Australopithecus afarensis. To this point, it is easy for us to understand the reason why Aitchison mentioned in her book that both Johnan and Edey would say: "put him (Homo habilis) on a subway and people would probably move to the other end of the car" (2000). Considering the fact that Homo habilis share both features of modern humans and ancient ape, scientists think the more suitable name for this kind of creature should be Pithecanthropus. As for the question

① Later discovery proves that apart from Australopithecus afarensis in Africa, there exists another kind of Homo habilis, which is named as Homo Rudolfensis and this kind of ancient pithecanthropus lived in African continent around two million years ago.

about whether Homo habilis (Pithecanthropus) have language or not, it depends on the way we define language and whether they have the biological condition which is suitable for language definition.

Another famous anthropologist, Leakey, thinks that the primal language of humans is a kind of protolanguage (1994). The earliest Homo, that is, Homo habilis which appeared more than two million years ago, should have their capability of using language. Leakey's evidence is that: in our modern human's brain, there are two areas, Broca's area and Wernick's area, for both language and tool's use. Moreover, two cerebral hemispheres are asymmetric and the left cerebrum, which controls language and our right hand's movement, is a little bigger than the right one. The traces of Broca's area and cerebral lateralization were discovered by Holloway in a cranium of a Homo habilis with more than two million years' age. What Leakey later concluded is that the language used by Homo habilis must be simple in its content and structure though, this kind of creature is definitely far more capable than Australopithecus afarensis.

Lieberman, however, stated that according to the latest study of many neurologists, the crucial part of controlling language is neither Broca's area and Wernick's area, nor cerebral cortex beneath the two areas, but many cerebral cortexes, nerve structure below and a series of lines of nerve which connects them all. Therefore, the discovery of Broca's area in fossils of ancient human's cranium may mean something but nothing significant. Lieberman also pointed out that cerebral lateralization is not a humans phenomenon alone, in fact, Peterson et al. (1978) noticed that this kind of phenomenon could be found in monkeys. It is well known (see Smith and Szathmary 1999) that typical protolanguage includes language used by kids less than two years old, language learned by children who are deprived of language environment, and pidgin and language learned by apes raised by humans. In protolanguage, there are words expressing concrete meaning, but there are no pure grammatical words indicating something concrete, such as "if" "that" "the" "when" "in" "not" etc. There is a basic word order, but from any aspect to see, there is no stratificational grammar. The basic unit of protolanguage is word, which is quite different from the alarming system of wild apes like vervet monkey. The former is a kind of sign, taking concept as signified and it can be used under the condition without any stimulation. The latter is a kind of signal and it has a fixed connection with certain stimulation outside. Objectively speaking, there is an insurmountable gap between the two. If we judge that this gap can be surmounted and a kind of protolanguage was mastered by Homo habilis only because the cranial capacity of it is bigger than that of Australopithecus afarensis, it is obvious that the evidence is not sufficient. In fact, researchers can also find out the phenomenon that dolphin can also speak out some simple "words" in a word order, but as for grammar, this kind of animal can do nothing about it.

The evolution of brain is a crucial must of human's language acquisition. However, it is not the sufficient condition. If we think that language is a vocal system used by following a certain regulation, then the evolution of organs of voicing is another crucial must of human's language acquisition. The time for language's formation is decided by the time that human's organs of voicing can evolve into a stage that he can produce certain sounds which cannot be mastered by other primates.

Vowel is the foundation of human's language. Vowels like [i], [a], [u] are the most fundamental ones. If humans cannot pronounce these sounds, he will face a great trouble in his pronunciation of clear sound. Without clear sound as signified of language sign, there is no possibility of language capability and even the capability of protolanguage. Along with Laitman and Reidenberg (1988), Lieberman (1991) thought that the main reason that humans can pronounce those three vowels is that larynx of humans is in a lower position of throat, much lower than those of primates. Consequently, the pipe of humans is much longer. However, the situation of newly-born baby of humans is quite different. The position of their larynx is the same as that of primate. After three months of their birth, the position of larynx will change, becoming lower and lower and gradually reaching the position of the adult human. Although larynx itself is a soft tissue and it cannot be fossilized, skull can provide research with a good opportunity. The shape of skull base has much to do with the position of larynx and it can even decide the exact position of this ogran. For humans adults, their skull bases are curved and their larynxes are in a low position, while those of newly-born babies are different. Their skull bases are flat and their larynxes are in a higher position, the same as those primates. In this way, we can judge the position of larynx via studying the shape of ancient human's skull basis and finally decide that the pipe can be a promise of producing those three crucial vowels, which is commonly used in humans language. According to the analysis of Laitman, Reidenberg and Lieberman (1991), the skull base of Australopithecus afarensis is flat, almost the same as that of chimpanzee. Thus, we can judge that the pipe of this ancient cousin does not share the capability of human's pronunciation and it is impossible for it to produce those key vowels. As for Homo habilis, the incomplete shape or excessive deformation of the skull base makes our conclusion in vain. It is not until one million and fifty thousand years ago, ancient Homo erectus' skull base started to curve, which marks that the position of its larynx changes a little and they can pronounce some sound as we humans can. Till the last three hundred thousand years, the curving degree of Archaic Homo sapiens could reach the same level of Homo sapiens sapiens, therefore, he can pronounce all sounds that we can produce. In another words, he can produce any sound in any language.

The research of paleoanthropologists on two most important preconditions provides us with an upper limit of the time that language appears: a certain protolanguage appeared more than one million five hundred thousand years ago, the period of Homo erectus. And the predecessor of modern language should appear at the time of ancient Homo sapiens, about thirty hundred thousand years ago.

1.2 Hypothesis of Eve and Origin of Modern Language

In the past, it was well known that modern humans in African and European continents are evolved from local Homo sapiens. This opinion is referred to as continuity theory or multi-regional evolution theory. In 1987, molecular biologists such as Cann (1987) and Wilson (1992) denied such opinion through their research on mitochondrial DNA of various modern humans worldwide. They came out with the thought that the birth land of modern humans' gene pool is in Africa. Because mitochondrial DNA is inherited through mother, according to the estimation of its evolutionary rate, the ancestor of all modern humans is a local female who lived in Africa around nine or eight million years ago. Later on, this theory is referred to as Eve hypothesis, which arouses a series of hot disputes about the origin of modern human. At present, the dispute continues. It seems that more scholars would like to accept this hypothesis because of the fact that not only the result (including blood pool, protein and enzyme) provided by Cavalli Sforza et al. happened to hold the same view, but also the fossils excavated from Africa and Israel supported the hypothesis. According to the introduction of Frayer et al (1993), at present the earliest fossil of modern humans was excavated in Ethiopia with an age of around three hundred thousand years. The age that can be determined is the fossil excavated from Israel and the ancestor's living period is around ninety to one hundred thousand years. These ancestor's cranial capacity is almost the same as modern humans, around 1430cm – 1550cm. ① Either from the cranial capacity or from the structure of pipe, these ancient humans should share the capability of language with modern humans. If all modern humans are descendants of Eve, and we suppose that those descendants reserved their language during the long history of stepping towards the whole earth and replacing local Archaic Homo sapiens, modern language possibly appeared after the emergence of early modern humans.

Hypothesis of Eve can solve a problem which keeps on bewildering European paleoanthropology, that is, the extinction of Homo neanderthalensis. This kind of ancient Homo has brilliant features. The cranial capacity of some can even surpass that of modern humans. Homo neanderthalensis were popular over Europe and Western Asia one hundred thirty thousand years ago. They enjoyed highly-developed culture and they could make tools and dress themselves. Later, they even understood the necessity of burying dead mem-

---

① Generally speaking, this ancient humans is referred to as Homo neanderthalensis. They are named after the spot of excavation-the valley of Neandertal, Germany. In the past, this kind of ancient humans is thought as a branch of Archaic Homo sapiens. However, most Paleoanthropologists think that Neandertals is a kind of independent humans race, different from Archaic Homo sapiens.

bers. However, this group of people who populated the earth once were replaced by Homo sapiens around thirty to forty thousand years ago. There are various explanations about the extinction of Homo neanderthalensis. One reasonable explanation goes like this: they are inferior to Homo sapiens in language. Through the analysis on their skull bases and jaws, Lieberman et al. (1971, 1972) thought that the pipe of this group of ancient humans is much closer to that of newly-born humans baby and other primates. They cannot produce those vowels like [i], [a], [u], thus they could not speak as we do. In consideration of their highly-developed culture, Lieberman (1984, 1991) acknowledged that Homo neanderthalensis probably owned a kind of protolanguage and communicated with each other. However, lack of a kind of "encoded discourse system", they could not speak out some words with our features as quickly as we do. Facing up with Homo sapiens owning "encoded discourse system", Homo neanderthalensis had no way to go but to be sorrowfully eliminated.

1.3 Non-Language-Culture Behavior and Origin of Language

Sophisticated central nerve system and organs of voicing which can pronounce all kinds of humans language are two essentials of modern humans language. However, these two are not the sufficient conditions. There are two fundamental components of humans language: verbal signs and regulations of using these signs. The sufficient condition of producing language is that some members of a community will name an object by using a certain speech sound, but they do not mean a concrete object in a context. If this condition cannot be satisfied, even the necessary condition is done, there is no possibility to produce language. If so, the communication system of our ancestor will still remain the level of animal's signal system. The sufficient condition of language production is a psychological and oral social behavior. Although this behavior cannot leave any trace for scientist to do research directly, they can investigate cultural behavior and its consequences related to language, expose the capability of language contained in these behaviors, and eventually acquaint the origin of language.

There are two important features in language. One is displacement and the other is creativity. Displacement enables us to allege objects outside concrete context, while creativity assures us to express infinitely various ideas with signs limited. Without language, displacement and creativity cannot continue and their sustainability is out of the question. If we can obtain this kind of capability of thinking through language, we can apply it to non language-culture activity and perform it in our daily life.

In the long process of evolution, tool making is a non language activity which represents displacement and creative thinking. Homo habilis is the first humans who can make tools. Although archeologists conclude these tools into choppers, scrapers, plates and balls, it is very difficult to say that these stone tools are made according to preset thoughts. Actually, every stone tool is made with its natural shape and only be roughly processed. The only thing that we can confirm is that after each strike the stone will be split into two parts, chip and core. Sometimes, chips are suitable for making scrapers and sometimes cores are easily made for chopping. From the tool of Homo habilis, it is obvious that the maker had no definite idea about what he or she wanted to make. Since there is no such a clear concept in the maker's mind, there is no possibility of language sign about it. What is more, during the long process from two million and three hundred thousand years to more than one million years time, Homo habilis did not upgrade their tools much. If they had language, they should have used it to accumulate and impart the knowledge of technique and the situation should not have been in this way.

After Homo habilis came out Homo erectus. It was more than one million and five hundred thousand year ago. Some paleoanthropologists, for example, Johnanson (1996) called Homo erectus in both Africa and Asia as Homo ergaster, although they have some similarities and differences in their evolutionary degree, time and their shapes. The reason why the name comes out is that they are more advanced than Homo habilis in tool-making. What Homo ergaster have made of different shapes, such as hand-ax, hacking knife, chopper or pickax. And the notable feature of these tools is that the process of tool-making is more complicated. Apparently, when Homo ergaster or Homo erectus were making tools, they had images of these tool in their mind. These images are equal to certain concrete concept expressed by words. It might be said that they expressed a certain idea via making a certain tool. Once the concept is formed, the quotation and expression of it can proceed without stimulation outside. For example, it is unnecessary for a Homo erectus to make out a hand-ax by seeing a hand-ax. At this point, tool-making is the same as discourse activity and it has the character of displacement. Because of the excavation of similar hand-ax in many different places, Gowlett (1984) brought about his idea: the shape's standardization of those hand-ax definitely tells us the fact that Homo erectus had mathematic ability and capability of language. Nevertheless, stone tools made by Homo ergaster or Homo erectus cannot reflect the creativity of language. In a long period from two million and three hundred thousand years to two hundred fifty thousand years, there were no obvious increase and improvement of the kind of tools and the technique of tool-making roughly remained the same level. From the above mentioned facts, we can draw a conclusion that even Homo ergaster or Homo erectus had their language capability, the capability is quite limited. And the limitation reaches such a degree that it constrained an efficient impartment and accumulation of knowledge and experience, even dragged behind the development of technique. It is hard to say that the limited language used by Homo ergaster or Homo erectus is a protolanguage or not. We may regard it as an initial language. Possibly, one important factor resulting in the slow development of Homo erectus' language is the underdevelopment of their organs of voicing, which became obstacles for them to pronounce all sounds of human.

According to the study of Gowlett (1992), around two hundred fifty thousand years ago, Homo habilis' technique in tool-making achieved a big progress, which presents to be a process in this way: Firstly, based on his or her own thought, the tool-maker would reshape one side of a stone core. Secondly started to chop the side when it turned to be the shape he or she wanted. Finally, the tool-maker could obtain the stone clips as he or she wished. This tool-making process shows plans and thoughts with obvious purpose. When it came to the period of mid Palaeolithic age, around one hundred thousand to forty thousand years ago, the sorts of stone tools became various. The hand-ax, which dominated the period before, was replaced by different reshaped choppers. The development and variety of tool not only reflects the displacement in tool-maker's thought, but also mirrors the creativity of toolmaker's thinking. All these actually are quite close to protolanguage pregnant. After the post Palaeolithic age, around forty thousand years ago, toolmaking technique advanced rapidly. The previous technique of stone clip was replaced by the one called stone edge. Based on the edged tool, advanced stone and bone tools for special purposes, such as graver, perforator, drillers, were made out one by one. The rapid advance of technique brings out the prosperity of culture. It is unimaginable that without highly-developed language as a media this kind of activity can be so prosperous. Davidson and Noble (1993) thought that as early as forty thousand years ago, humans came across the ocean and landed in the continent of Australia. Undoubtedly, the event proves the existence of language. Possibly, those early colonists used drafts and the behavior of draft-making share one common ground with the behavior of language. That is, integrating some basic units under certain forms, then making out a bigger unit.

Apart from the development of technique, symbolic presentation also proves the existence of language. Artistic expressions, such as painting, sculpture and body-adornment, appear much later. At present, all works discovered are made about thirty five hundred thousand years ago (Bahn, 1992). In addition, the meaning of sacrificial objects are worthy of research. Once Lieberman (1998) pointed out that archaeologists discovered a lot of sacrificial objects from the tombs excavated in Israel which belong to the Homo habilis living around one hundred thousand years ago. Those bear skulls or horns of deer have marked a significant step of human. And from the tomb sacrificial objects, we can deduce that humans at that time started to think about the meaning of death and life and they formed a certain idea about the world afterlife. Actually, this kind of abstract thinking must turn to the help of a certain advanced language.

Combining the achievements of paleoanthropology with those of molecular biology and archaeology, we can draw a conclusion that humans had some highly developed language one hundred thousand to forty thousand years ago. About forty thousand year ago, those protolanguages started to enrich themselves in both vocabulary and grammar, and gradually marched into the era of modern language.

1.4 Formation of Word Order

Supposing that Australopithecus afarensis had an alarm system as the vervet monkey does, we can see three big leaps in the process of the evolution from a kind of communicative system into modern humans language. The first leap is the appearance of proto-words. It marks that the communicative system of Homo has changed itself from the signal foundation into sign foundation. The second leap is the appearance of the formation of word order, which marks the birth of protolanguage. The third leap is the presence of some grammatical means, such as function words and reflection. Definitely, this leap marks the transition of protolanguage to modern language.

There might be various sources of proto-words. And the number of them is quite limited, no more than dozens. Because those proto-words are used alone, their functions and meanings rely on context to a great extent (Aitchison, 2000). It cannot be said that these proto-words used alone consist of language, even protolanguage because language requires grammar. Word order is the most basic and common grammatical means. However, proto-words are used alone, and there is no word order in them. With the enrichment of vocabulary, different words should be combined under a certain rules and in this way grammar is established. Thus, protolanguage comes into being. With the fixation of word order, other grammatical means, mainly functions words and reflection, are gradually evolved. It can be said that the appearance of every new grammatical means marks a leap of language. After many leaps, protolanguage evolves into modern language step by step. So to speak, language evolution is mainly composed of the evolution of three grammatical means: word order, function words and reflection, apart from the enrichment and evolution of vocabulary.

In English, the term "word order" is quite obvious. Literally, it means the order of words' arrangement. However, to understand this term in this way is of a narrow sense. If we understand it in a broad sense, the term "word order" includes the arrangement of grammar ingredients, such as "subject" "verb" "object" "adverbial modifier" and "complement". Therefore, the term "word order" is actually "syntax order". For the convenience of narration, here I want to differentiate "word order" with "syntax order". The former means the order among words and the latter indicates the order among different grammatical constituents.

The words "subject" "verb" "object" are regarded as three basic constituents of sentence, which take different order in different lauguages. According to the differences among different languages, linguists have named different languages with different orders, such as "SOV, Subject + Object + Verb" "SVO, Subject + Verb + Object" "VSO, Verb + Subject + Object" "VOS, Verb + Object + Subject" and "OVS, Object + Verb + Subject". The research of language origin should account for the word order of protolanguage and the reason why the word order will be diverse in different languages. Because of the lack of direct evidence, we can only deduce the primal order of language with the help of limited clues. Aitchison(2000) introduced three clues: Firstly, the word order used by chimpanzee Nim and Bonobo Kanzi, which accepted a certain language training. Secondly, the word order used by a three-year-old kid named Vincent who has learned signed language before. Thirdly, the word order in human's mind set.

There are some obvious tendencie in chimpanzee Nim's word order, such as, words about food always ahead of other words; "more" in the collocation of two words always in a prior position. But we can notice the tendency of instability in Nim's language. If we use the three grammatical constituents as "subject" "verb" "object", we will immediately notice that there exist many orders like "OSV" "OVS" "SV" "VS" "VO" and "OV". This phenomenon shows that Nim is unaware of the way to distinguish "subject" and "verb" from each other and confirm their order according to the "agent-patient" relations. It is more noticeable that in the word order used by Nim there is no trace of the most common order as "SOV" and "SVO" in mordern language. By contrast, Kanzi's situation is quite different. It has not only learned "VO" order from its English partner, but also by itself created a way of combining verb with gesture to indicate the agent. The reason why Kanzi is slightly better than Nim is probably that this bonobo's trainer not only used a human-ape pedagogy, but also utilized keyboard sign as a language media. As for the aspect of exploring the word order of protolanguage, the case of Vincent cannot prove much when he is learning oral language. The basic word order used by this kid is "SVO", and this is exactly the order of English. Some sentences made by Vincent are quite strange, like "You house you", which means "Can those buses take you home?". The way of making such strange sentence is noticeable, probably because Vincent's capability of oral expression is far behind his capability of thinking which is developed by means of signed language learning. There is a common ground in Nim, Kanzi and Vincent, that is, what they have learned at the beginning is not oral language.

Supposing that the primal language of humans is signed language but not oral language, the word order used by them, especially by Nim, will help us greatly to reconstruct the word order or syntax order of protolanguage. The question is, however, none can prove that before humans oral language there existed a period of signed language.

The Mind set theory is indeed a copy of Noam Chomsky's "universal grammar" theory. This theory insists that there exists an innate cognitive structure in humans brain. Both the way that humans recognize bigger categories like man, material, act and event and the rule that humans use to combine these categories with each other are controlled by our cognitive structure. Thus, some model of thinking are formed. Language is established on the foundation of humans cognitive structure. Because of the two rules of "the priority of agent" and "act-patient junction", most of languages all over the world have either word order as "SVO" or word order as "SOV". What word to take is decided by the word order in those native speakers' minds. However, only by means of the word order as "A is ahead of B", we cannot say that the principle tells the innate thinking way of human. For example, crying is an innate behavior and any normal baby will cry at the time of his or her birth. In other words, the principle of "the priority of the living " and "the priority of agent" cannot be obeyed by all people.

Based on clues at present, we cannot draw any conclusion on the word order and syntax order of protolanguage. The only thing that we can do is to speculate that the primal word order is probably very unstable. When some word order becomes more and more common and widely accepted by members in a community, people start to obey the principle consciously and the word order or syntax order are set. If we want to study which word order is the earliest one, the best way for us to follow is to find several babies and teach them only vocabulary but not phrases or sentences, then we probably can see what kind of tendency they will show when they can speak out sentences with two or three words.

1.5 Grammaticalization

Although several dozens of words can bring out infinite permutation and combination, actually inside of a language unit, the permutation and combination made by all constituents are quite limited. Furthermore, the grammar and meaning of language expressed by word order is more limited. In the process of language evolution, other grammatical means will develop in order to satisfy the requirement of signification. Among these means, the change of function word and reflection is the most common way.

Preposition may be an early one in function words. In fact, there are "preposition" and "postposition". Because preposition and postposition express the direction and possession, which are of great importance in the basic cognitive activity of human, therefore, this kind of function word can be divided into "pre-" and "post-". There are several characteristics in both "preposition" and "postposition": First, it is extensively distributed and there is no language without this kind of function word. Second, there are limitedly numbered and there are less than dozens of preposition and postposition in any language. Third, it is mainly used for two words' connection and tells the relation between them. Fourth, this kind of function word is usually transformed from notional words, such as verb and noun. Preposition and postposition are kind of grammatical word. The transformation from notional word into function word is a kind of grammaticalization. It is worth discussing the time when the earliest words prepositionalized and the way how they are prepositionalized or postpositionalized because these have much to do with the origin of modern language.

Among reflections, all notional words may experience the reflective change. Aitchison (2000) concentrated on the discussion of the reflective change and origin of "tense" "aspect" and "mood" in both Pidgin and Creole. It is possible that Aitchison wanted to make her book more readable, so she did not use "reflection"—the term of linguistics but use a more common term—"verbal attachment". In addition, she also borrowed a new term—"-gram", which is coined by Bybee et al. (1994), to express a grammatical sign. In Creole, the attached constituents of verb is to mark the mood of anterior, non-punctual and non-real. The same goes with preposition and postposition, for these attached constituents are notional words at beginning. Usually, there is not only one word which can play the role of candidate for one grammatical sign. To begin with, the use of these constituents is quite inflexible, and it will be used whenever it is necessary. Afterwards, when it goes through the process of meaning-breaching, transformation and re-explanation, one word eliminates other candidates, turning out to be a constituent which must be attached to a verb. In this way, a language sign is finally set.

Aitchison (2000) thought that the grammaticalization of both Pidgin and Creole is the same as other languages and is probably similar to primal humans language, except the faster speed. It is undeniable that the evidence provided by Pidgin and Creole is very inspirable for us to understand the primal grammaticalization in humans language, however, such evidence cannot replace the trace made by historical linguists for grammaticalization itself.

1.6 Spread of Language and Trace of Historical Linguists of Language

Language is a behavior of humans. Wherever humans go, they will spread their language. In other words, the spead of language is the spread of humans. As I mentioned earlier, fossils of Homo habilis defined by anatomy were first found in Africa, and similar ones were found in Israel. In Europe, the earliest humans appeared around forty thousand years ago. With highly developed stone tool-making technique and language advantage, they dominated the area once controlled by local Homo neanderthalensis. Because of the fact that in shape and technique the earliest European Homo habilis is very much close to those who lived in Mid-East more than fifty thousand years ago, and the latter in shape is similar to Homo habilis living in Africa and Mid-East one hundred thousand years ago, we can draw a conclusion that African Homo habilis went out of Africa around one hundred thousand years to fifty thousand years ago. They arrived in Europe forty thousand years ago and finally became ancestors of modern Europeans.

According to the "going out of Africa" theory, other groups of Homo habilis first turned to east direction and then arrived in Indian sub-continent and then Indochina after they left Africa. Later on, this group was divided into two. One was ahead for the south and eventually reached Pacific southern island area about fifty thousand years ago; another group went to the north, entering east Asia around sixty to forty thousand years ago. There they replaced local Homo habilis and at last became the ancestor of modern east Asians. Afterwards, some Homo habilis from North-East Asia came across Bering Strait and went into North America around thirty thousand to ten thousand years ago. As we can see today, their footprints widely extended to every corner of the whole American continent.

The ancestor of modern Europeans is Homo habilis from Africa, and there is no doubt about this point. However, as for the issue about whether the ancestor of Asians is also from Africa or not, there exist serious disagreements. In short, both "Eve hypothesis" and "going out of Africa" theory have evidence from either molecular biology or humans genetics, however, they lack strong support from paleoanthropology, especially archaeology. As a consequence, there is no evidence which can prove that Asian Homo habilis was replaced by Homo habilis from outside. On the other hand, paleoanthropologists have not discovered any fossils that can be confirmed as ones of Homo habilis living one hundred to sixty thousand years ago, therefore, none can prove that the way of Asian Homo habilis changing into modern humans is a continuous process of evolution.

The Origin of language should be included in language history. In this case, the study on language (including humans language) origin is one mission of historical linguists. Nevertheless, because historical linguistics takes language itself as its research object, it has to excavate evidence from language interior. In available range of time, this kind of evidence seriously controls the development of historical linguistics. Traditionally, this discipline narrows its research range into less than ten thousand years and it will face up with an embarrassment once the time is beyond ten thousand years. Frankly speaking, the reason is simple. When a language is divided into two parts geographically, both of the two will evolve respectively. And ten-thousand-year time will totally change a language and make it out of recognition from all aspects. Consequently, the genetic relationship of the two evolved from a language will be unrecognizable. In a given time range, historical linguists can either study a certain language's origin or stimulate protolanguage of a certain language family, but they cannot trace the origin of humans language. Nonetheless, in the past fifty years some scholars have made a breakthrough and free themselves from the yoke of traditional historical comparative linguistics, keeping on tracing the common origin of various language family and even humans language.

Aitchison summed up the methods used by linguists tracing language origin as the following three and they are comparison of clans, comparison of regions and comparison of similarities.

Comparison of clans confirms the relations of various languages mainly through the comparison of cognates in different languages. It is the method used by traditional historical comparative linguistics and its most well known achievement is the confirmation of the relations among most of European languages. What is more, it has stimulated primal Indo-European language five thousand years ago. There is no more disagreement or dispute about this aspect, and the only aspect debated is the spot of Indo-European language origin. Is it in the grassland of Ukraine or Anatolia (Turkey today)? In the 60s of the 20 th century, two scholars from former Soviet Union discovered over seven hundred cognates through the comparison of Indo-European language, Uralic language, Altaic language, Afro-Asian language and Dravidian language (Rulhen, 1996). The two scholars thought that all these languages they had studied have a common ancestor—Nostratic. Later on, more scholars put forward a language-Super Nostratic, whose coverage is wider (Aitchison, 2000).

Comparison of regions is to find out some irrelevant features of language. For example, the differences between the first person pronoun singular form as "we" and subject-object form as "we"; and also the differences between inalienable possession "my mother (wo ma)" and alienable possession "my horse (wo ma)". This comparison investigates the distribution of these language phenomenon in different languages all over the world and deduces language's evolution and extension according to the geographical distribution of these features. Nichols is the most saliently representative among those scholars. She found out that the two features mentioned above have a kind of tendency, that is, geographically, the tendency of gradually becoming denser from the West (west Europe) to the East (east Asia and even America). For this phenomenon, her explanation is that this tendency exactly reflects the migration of humans from the West to the East and the following extension of language. She believed that the farther east, the less obvious is Western language's influence and the more feature of ancient language are preserved. Based on this, Nichols asserted that any feature appearing frequently in the Eastern language but not the Western language must be very ancient, more than tens of thousands years old.

Comparison of similarities is referred to as "lucky dip" by Aitchison (2000). In other words, by means of consulting dictionaries researchers find out some words similar in form and meaning among languages without any relations. Based on these similarities, they establish a certain relation of clans and try to construct a common ancestor of all languages. Aitchison was quite dismissive, criticizing it for either its ignorance of language's occasional correspondence or its possibility of being tested by time. In Aitchison's opinion, the method used by Ruhlen in the study of language origin is exactly this kind of method. However, Aitchison's opinion is not fair. In fact, the method used by Ruhlen is almost the same as comparison of clans in terms of principle. The cognates he studied in different language families are not from dictionaries, but based on the achievements of his predecessors, especially Greenberg (2000). According to taxonomy and historical comparison used by Greenberg and other scholars, about five thousand languages existing now can be categorized into twelve language branches. However, Ruhlen moved further on the foundation of those twelve languages. Through the comparison of the cognates from those branches, Ruhlen found out scores of roots, like "-tik (means finger and one)" "-pal (means two)" "-kaka (means brother)" and "-ac'wa (means water)" and so on, widely exist in these various languages. The existence of these roots makes him believe that there is a common ancestor of all existing language worldwide. On the foundation of roots of those cognates, Ruhlen put forward and proved the solo origin of language. It cannot be said that roots of those cognates discovered by this scholar are of no ingredients occasionally similar or far-fetched. However, his discovery cannot be simply commented as "occasionally similar" or "far-fetched". If we believe that we can find out some traces, there is no other linguistic method more scientific and more strict except Ruhlen's way.

So far, we have seen that language, a gift which is always taken for granted by us, is so complicated and so fascinating that it is worth of infinite research with humans evolution. Any scornful attitude towards its function and essence, especially towards its superficially simple rules and uses will be ridiculed by experts.

1.7 What is Redundancy?

From the review and data mentioned above, the fact that language plays a crucial role in communication is affirmative. In another words, humans use language to exchange information, ideas, thoughts and this behavior, without any doubt, accelerates the evolution of mankind. Since language is for information exchange purpose, it needs to follow certain rules. First and foremost, efficiency of information exchange is of the top priority of any language. However, it is interesting that in practical use of language, we humans frequently use more words, phrases and even sentences to express ourselves than the real information exchange requires. And this kind of redundant information is referred to as an strange but at the same time normal language phenomenon, that is, redundancy.

The concept of redundancy originally derives from Information Theory, which has given a momentous impetus to various studies in many fields. In linguistics, redundancy is not a brand-new topic. The term "redundancy" often invokes negative associations not only to laity but also to some professional linguists. People tend to attach importance to "least effort" in their works. When referring to redundancy, they often relate it to derogatory words such as "uselessness" "wordiness" and "waste of effort". What is more, quite a few dictionaries provide a derogative definition that stains the functions of redundancy. In spite of this, many researches on redundancy have been carried out. And in recent years people have gradually got a comprehensive understanding of redundancy with the further study on it in translation, psychology, pragmatics and other fields. As a matter of fact, redundancy is an intrinsic feature of language and it exists in all levels of language, from basic levels such as phonetics and morphology to high levels such as communication.

Redundancy, a prevailing phenomenon in language, is abundantly found in all kinds of linguistic communication. As Nida (1963) says, "In order to combine efficiency of communication with an effective guarantee against distortion by noise and other factors, language tend to be about 50 percent redundant. Any message can be communicated through any channel, but it may be necessary to lengthen the message, that is, to take more time to communicate it if the channel is too restricted."

With regard to redundancy, there are many definitions. The following are the normal explanations:

1. The state of being redundant; a superfluity; something redundant or excessive; a needless repetition in language; excessive wordiness.

2. The state of being redundant; a superfluity; something redundant or the duplication of components or circuits to provide survival of the total system in case of failure of single components.

3. The state of being redundant; a superfluity; something redundant or the duplication of parts of a message to guard against transmission errors.

4. The state of being redundant; a superfluity; something redundant or ("mostly British") the state of being unemployed because one's job is no longer necessary; the dismissal of such an cmployee; a layoff.

Now, let us have a look at the explanations for redundancy in some famous dictionaries: In *Webster's New World Dictionary of the American Language*, "redundant" is described as: 1. more than enough; overabundant; excess; superfluous. 2. using more words than needed; wordy. 3. unnecessary to the meaning: said of words and affixes. And redundancy is explained as follows: 1. the state or quality of being redundant; superfluity. 2. a redundant quality; overabundance. 3. the use of redundant words. 4. the part of a redundant statement that is superfluous.

In *The World Book Dictionary*, redundancy is given such meanings: 1. more than needed. 2. a redundant thing, part, or amount. 3. the use of too many words for the same idea; wordiness. 4. the part of communication that can be omitted without loss of essential information.

In *Oxford Dictionary of the English Language*, redundancy is defined as: 1. In general usage, more of anything than is (strictly) needed, usually resulting from repetition or duplication, pleonasm or tautology. In the sentence they also visited us last week too, either also or too is redundant, because both words express the same idea. 2. Technically, both repetition of information (or the inclusion of extra information so as to reduce errors in understanding messages) and part of a message which can be eliminated without loss of essential information.

And in *Routledge Dictionary of Language and Linguistics*, the definition of redundancy is: 1. In general, excess information, that is, information expressed more than once and which hence could easily be forgone in some occurrences. However, since linguistic communication is constantly hampered by disruptive noises, idiolectal and other variation, inattention and misinterpretation, language has developed into a means of communication characterized by a great degree of redundancy. This is apparent on all levels of linguistic description, perhaps most clearly in the plethora of morphological markings and in lexical repetition. Redundancy is also intentionally used for rhetorical purposes. 2. In Information Theory, redundancy correlates in a statistically verifiable manner with the probability of occurrence of the particular element of information, that is, the more probable the occurrence of a particular sign, or the more frequently a particular expression is used, the less information value it has.

From those definitions above, we are often reminded of its negative effects such as uselessness, wordiness and waste of effort. However, redundancy is a prevailing phenomenon in language and in many linguistic situations it is not avoided at all. That is to say, redundancy does not mean unnecessary, and the definition in these dictionaries is biased. Therefore, as the correlative consequence, in the following chapters, the book will examine the great value and indispensability of redundancy in certain contexts.

Since the proposal of the concept of redundancy, many researches have been done about it in different fields. Therefore, many other definitions are given from different perspectives. They also can be divided into two schools—a micro-defining scheme (definition 1 and 2) and a macro-defining scheme (definition 3 and 4). And each will be critically examined for its strengths and weaknesses.

Definition 1: Redundancy is the property of texts that allows us to predict missing symbols from the context.

This definition, which regards redundancy as the property of texts was first proposed by Carroll in 1964. It points out two defining features of redundancy. Firstly, predictability. A redundant linguistic unit can be used to predict some information contained in a message. If some symbols are missing, it can be guessed from other units. That is to say, the information that contained in the redundant units has already existed in other symbols and they are a kind of repetition for each other. Secondly, contextuality. A random organized text will be with low redundancy but nonsense, while a successful and meaningful text must be well organized and contain redundancy which can help to make the information clearly understood. The redundancy not only can be a word but also can be a clause, sentence and even a paragraph. This means redundancy is contextual.

Although predictability in context is a feature of redundancy and can be workable in some situation, it is just one of the features and infeasible for lots of cases because not all of the redundancies are repetitions. For example, verbal fillers are a kind of redundancy which will be given detailed explanation in the next part of this chapter.

Definition 2: Redundancy is a property of languages, codes and sign systems, which arises from a superfluity of rules.

Cherry (1978) developed his own defining scheme on the basis of Carroll's definition. In his opinion, redundancy comes from the superfluity of all kinds of rules, from words level to text level, which guarantees the accuracy of the message. All the linguistic units should obey a certain rule to organize a meaningful sequence. For instance, "there are four apples in the table". Here the plural concept has been expressed three times: "are" "four" and the suffix "-s", among which just "four" contains meaning and the other two are the need for grammar rules in English. In Chinese, abstract nouns like 任务 (task), 工作 (work), 问题 (problem), and 事业 (career) have no exact meaning but they are indispensable in Chinese sentences. We can say the existence of those words is just for the requirement of Chinese syntax. Therefore, these rules are redundant. As the cases show, language is designed in such a way that the various rules duplicate and supplement one another to ensure that communication is not hampered, interrupted or completely halted.

However, Cherry's definition is also imperfect because rules in language are not the sole reason for redundancy, which can also be caused by pragmatic and rhetorical purposes. For instance:

A: What did your sister buy at Sears yesterday?

B: She bought a red dress, she bought a green dress, and she bought a blue dress.

In the above example, *she bought* is used for three times. It is the redundant elements in the expression because we can only say "she bought too many things". But in this certain context, it is not redundant at all because the speaker needs to use the repetition to abreact his or her dissatisfied mood. Hence, Cherry's owing redundancy to mere superfluity of grammar or syntactical rules is incomplete and his definition only presents a partial picture of redundancy.

Definition 3: Grammatical redundancy is internal to the language system, systematic and obligatory; whereas contextual redundancy is voluntary. Contextual redundancy involves the judgment of the speaker concerning the receptors background or it may simply be used to achieve certain rhetorical effects.

This definition, we think, is a breakthrough made by Gillette & Wit (1998). It classifies linguistic redundancy into what they call "contextual redundancy" and "grammatical redundancy". And it points out redundancy plays a role in grammar, semantics, syntax and other aspects of language. However, it just gives a feature of redundancy but does not define what redundancy on earth is and through this definition we still cannot distinguish redundant information from other information. Therefore, there is still a fly in the ointment.

Definition 4: Redundancy is the difference between the received information and transmitted information. This definition is proposed by Wang Dechun (2001) in his research of modern rhetoric. He points out that if the information received by the receiver is more than that sent by the transmitter, there is redundancy. Redundancy can be caused by the misunderstanding of the intended meaning, which related to the social factors such as culture, psychology and even people's personality. Generally speaking, all forms of coding that are not consistent with the context may cause hidden information which will become redundant information when it is not what the transmitter intends. (Wang, 2001)

One distinguishing point of this definition is that it takes receivers into consideration during the production process of redundancy. However, this makes the definition too subjective to recognize because there are too many factors that will affect people in interpreting the original message. Different people have different opinions about one thing, not to mention people from different culture backgrounds. Apparently, there is no need to require everyone hold the same idea on one message. Therefore, we cannot call this difference redundancy.

本章主要是对人类进化史、进化理论、动物的认知和交流以及人类语言研究的概述。从语言的起源、进化历史出发,让读者对语言有一个总体的了解。进而指出在漫长的语言演变过程中,不可避免地会出现一些特殊的语言现象,例如冗余。并指出我们应该科学、客观地看待这种语言现象,以及对此进行研究的必要性。

Chapter 2 Literature Review

For a long time, linguists have had a lot of studies and debates on redundancy, and have got their own opinions. Quite a few scholars hold the idea that redundancy is negative. They believe that redundancy will only impede communicative activities since it violates Cooperative Principle and goes against Economy Principle. Because it is said that brevity is the soul of wit, when it comes to redundancy, we are often reminded of its negative effects such as uselessness, wordiness and waste of effort. However, in many discourses or vocal use situations, redundancy is not avoided at all. On the contrary, it is largely employed to achieve certain pragmatic purposes and rhetorical effects. This book holds that redundancy does have positive functions in spite of its negative effects in some cases, so a good knowledge of redundancy and its functions is of great significance in understanding and using language effectively.

The previous studies on redundancy can be categorized into two groups: microscopic point of view and macroscopic point of view. The former only refers to the language signs system itself, which is the basic level of language;

while the latter mainly discusses redundancy in language use process such as language teaching, translation and communication. This book will study redundancy from the perspective of pragmatics, a macroscopic point of view. It is observed that, in the process of language use, people consciously or unconsciously use redundancy to achieve certain pragmatic purposes, rhetorical effects or textual functions. Although some studies have tackled redundancy from the aspect of pragmatic functions, few attempts have been made to interpret it according to pragmatic theories systematically. Rhetorical effects of redundancy have been mentioned but there is no detailed analysis, letting alone the analysis of it in text. In fact, besides all kinds of functions, we found that there are some implicit reasons for the existence of redundancy. Therefore, this book tries to meet these challenges and attempts to exploit the implicit reasons. All the work done here is with the hope to prove the value of redundancy in pragmatic area and to get a more comprehensive understanding of this language phenomenon. Before detailed discussion of the essence, functions and influential factors of language redundancy, it is necessary for us to have an overview of this aspect because the achievements of the predecessors will give us a great help from all aspects.

The concept of redundancy was first put forward by Claude Shannon in 1948 in Information Theory, which is a branch of the statistical theory of communication science. According to Shannon (1949), "if the channel is noisy, it is not in general possible to reconstruct the original message or the transmitted signal." Then redundancy must be introduced in a proper way to combat the noise involved. Since any channel cannot be noise free but full of errors, redundancy can make it possible to correct such errors. A channel with redundancy is of vital importance in correcting errors and amplifying information when transmitted messages have encountered noise during the transmission. A redundant element is one that is not necessary to the sense of the message but serves to indicate errors if the message does not agree with a previous part of the message. That is to say, redundancy is a way to ensure understanding and to avoid misunderstanding. A message entirely without redundancy may contain the maximum amount of information but can not be corrected if it is corrupted in some way, because there is no space material to check with (Steven, 1992).

Since Shannon put forward the concept of redundancy, there have been a lot of researches at home and abroad. They can be divided into two categories: microscopic analysis and macroscopic analysis. In microscopic aspect, the researches mainly touch upon the basic levels of language. Among them the most relevant ones are on morphology and phonetics, while from macroscopic point of view, researches related to redundancy are mainly in the fields of translation, language teaching and communication.

2.1 Microscopic Analysis of Redundancy

2.1.1 Redundancy in morphology

Nicolaci-da-Costa and Harris (1983) have done a research about redundancy within the boundary of a sentence when the children are playing a role of hearers. They want to study whether children find redundancy helpful or not when listening to other people. Their experiments show that children's comprehension of sentential number is powerfully aided by information involving differently, but not by sheer repetition of the same marker. For example, in the sentence "That boy drives his car.", the singular information is conveyed five times through different syntactic markers, namely, demonstrative (that), nouns (boy, car), present tense (drives) and possessive (his). There is a wider range of markers to choose from in this sentence, so the children have a better chance of picking out a marker or markers they have already mastered and thus these markers are an aid to children's comprehension. However, as the sentence "The sheep jumps, runs and plays." is concerned, it does not have any facilitative effect upon little children's understanding if they don't know the suffix "s" added to "jump" "run" and "play" is to convey singular meaning.

2.1.2 Redundancy in phonetics

Xu Shenghuan is the scholar who does research on redundancy at a very early time in China. According to his understanding, redundancy is one of characteristics of language in which redundant information and effective information co-exist and people apply it consciously or unconsciously in the process of language use. He uses the formula R = 1-Hoo/Ho, proposed by Claude Shannon, to calculate the degree of redundancy of English letters. (R stands for redundancy; H stands for entropy, i. e. degree of uncertainty; Ho is the amount of information that is actually achieved. One minus the relative entropy is the redundancy.) For instance, there are 26 letters in English. Plusing a 'zero letter' as 'space', there are 27 in all. Theoretically the maximum amount of information of each letter is Ho = 1og 27 = 1.4314. To reach this, it is required that 26 + 1 letters always appear at the same frequency. Empirically, we know it is not true. According to some experimental statistics, he finally gets the degree of redundancy in English letters: 67%-80%, which is so high that the following passage with some letters left out, is still readable:

D—M—H—,

Whi—w—w—h—ing lun—la—w—, me—t—ned—jo—in ou—Lon—off—,—ve n—w—en aut—ed t—off—i—t—y—. (*Linguaphone English Course* 2, Lesson 28)

There are 107 letters (not counting space) in all, and 57 words are left out, but it is still guessable to a person with certain English proficiency. For instance, the word before it may be a variant of 'be', so 'were' is possible, and 'were' denotes past time. The two words before the comma may be 'last week'. There are only two one-letter words in this passage, and in English either 'I' or 'a' is possible, and 'me—t—ned' must be a verb, so the two words are 'I' and 'a' in order. The whole passage is not difficult to guess in this way. (The original version reads: Dear Mr. Hun, while we were having lunch last week, I mentioned a job in London office. I have now been authorized to offer it to you.)

In Tang Jianjun's article (2001) about redundancy, he also points out that in English phonetics there is a great deal of redundancy. In 48 phonemes of English, only 9 are used in a highest frequency. The occurrence of 26 letters is with a great disparate frequency, among which the difference between the highest ones and the lowest ones can be 100 times. So the chances for letters to co-occur are not the same at all. For example, letter "t" and "h" are probable to co-occur while letter "t" and "k" are not likely to appear together in normal occasions. The prefix and the suffix of English words are often consonants, which contains more information in general. Therefore, in many sentences, even some vowels are omitted in a word, we still can guess the meaning. For example, the following sentence can be understood: MST PPL HV LTTL DFFCLTYN RDNG THSSNTNC (most people have little difficulty in reading this sentence). Based on this, Tang thinks that in some cases vowels are redundant in words.

2.2 Macroscopic Analysis of Redundancy

2.2.1 Redundancy and translation

Eugene A. Nida is the father of American translation theory, and he is the first one to take redundancy into consideration in translation. As he says: (1963) In order to combine efficiency of communication with an effective guarantee against distortion by noise and other factors, language tend to be about 50 percent redundancy. Any message can be communicated through certain channel, but it may be necessary to lengthen the message, that is, to take more time to communicate it if the channel is too restricted. He also thinks that in order to get the exact meaning of the author, in translation, "the relationship between receiver and translated text should be the same with that between original receiver and original text". However, in normal sense, the information channel of translated text readers is often smaller than that of original readers. In this situation, the translator should lengthen the message, that is, to add some redundant information to make sure the original meaning can get fully understood.

In China, Liao Qiyi (1996) probes into the possible application of redundancy to find out ways to lighten the TL semantic and formal communication loads by adding certain redundancy in Chinese-English and English-Chinese translation. According to him, language communication is essentially a transmission of information. Translation is an interlingual communication, in which there exists a great disparity of language structure and culture background between original and target language. Therefore, it is easy to destroy the intrinsic balance of information channel in each language. The main reason, except the pure mistakes in comprehension and expression, comes from the difference of intrinsic redundancy in two languages. Liao proposes two methods to make a balance for the redundancy: one from syntax and the other from semantics. In syntax, the most useful ways are supplication of the omitted elements, change of the language structure and separation of the whole language units, while in terms of semantics, the effective ways are: adding some words with the same meaning to the original language, replacing it with some descriptive words, pointing out the implication meaning and providing the culture background knowledge.

2. 2. 2 Redundancy and language teaching

Gui Shichun (1980), a famous scholar in China, conducts a research on redundancy and language teaching. In his opinion, redundancy can be divided into two categonies: redundancy existing in English signs system and redundancy existing in the process of language use. After his discussion of the manifestations of English redundancy, he analyzes the effect of redundancy in English from the perspective of foreign language teaching. First, redundancy can help us to understand the language teaching process. Children always follow some certain rules when they acquire their mother tongue. The order for their acquisition is from content words to language structure and then to change of word formation. From this procedure, we can get some light in our foreign language teaching: 1. In language acquisition, children first focus on the content of the message rather than the language signs; while in our traditional foreign language teaching, teachers always put much emphasis on language symbols at first, even treat it as the final goal. 2. The occasions for children to acquire a language are various and full of redundant language materials; while in our foreign language classes, the language materials are selected and processed carefully, which are not the ones in real language use. 3. There is a difference of redundancy in different languages. Some phenomenon which is redundant in one language may not be the same case in other languages. So teachers should have a clear understanding of redundancy in different languages to know exactly what the difficult and important points are in foreign language teaching.

Second, the comprehension of redundancy can help us to improve the basic language skills: listening, speaking, reading and writing. In listening process, students should learn how to grasp the content of the message and pay little attention to or even ignore the redundant information. In speaking practice, we can learn how to use redundant words such as verbal fillers to make us more natural. In reading, redundancy can decrease the uncertainty speech of the information and help us to get the exact meaning, while in writing, different writing styles require different degree of redundancy. Generally speaking, redundancy is arranged in descending order of degree in the following continuum:

telecommunications →face-to-face talk →informal writings →formal writing →abstract of a paper →headlines →telegrams →shorthand (Gui, 1980).

2. 2. 3 Redundancy and communication

Turk and Kirkman (1989) take the consideration of redundancy into communication. They think redundancy is an important aspect of communication that compensates for any loss of data in the transition between stages. In their communication model, they highlight an important aspect of redundancy in communication which other models seem to overlook. They identify four steps at which data is transferred from one medium to another. At each step, part of the information, facts or ideas may be lost. Information is potentially lost in this way (see diagram 2. 1): first, when the message is transferred from facts to language; second, when it is transferred from language to spoken/ written words; third, when it is transferred from spoken/ written words to language in another mind; and fourth, when it is transferred out of that language into stored information. In other words, redundancy is present at all four steps of data transition instead of at merely one step as has been often assumed, for example, from language to spoken words. In order to transmit the information completely and exactly, redundancy is needed at all of the four steps. Wang Hong (2000) examines and explores the distribution and the active roles of redundancy from the view of pragmatics. In the meantime he gives some suggestions for students to develop their ability to utilize redundancy in the daily communication. According to him, redundancy can be divided into four types: repetition, circumlocution, verbal fillers and phatic communion.

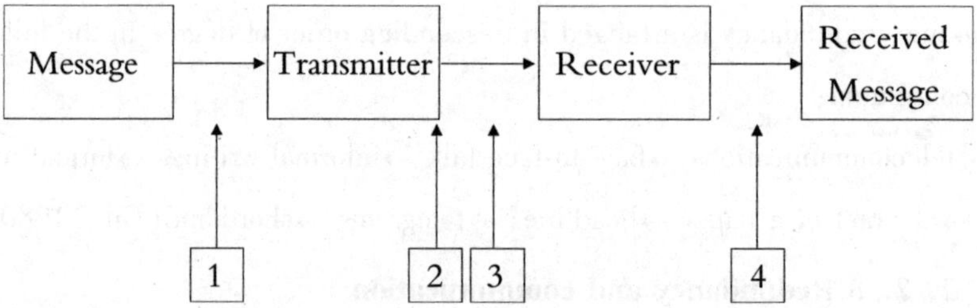

Diagram 2. 1 Four points at which a message is transferred

(Turk & Kirkman, 1989)

As I have mentioned before, repetition refers to doing, saying or writing the same thing more than once. The recurrence of processes, structures, elements and motifs is fundamental to communication in general and to language in particular. Such repetition occurs at all levels, starting with rhythm. Repetition further includes repetition of form and repetition of meaning. Circumlocution, also called periphrasis, in rhetoric, is a wordy and indirect way of saying something. In other words, circumlocution refers to the use of many words where fewer would do, so it is regarded as a kind of redundancy. Such usage is often obscure, officious, pompous, authoritarian and intimidating. Verbal filler is an inclusive term here. It includes those meaningless sounds used to fill the gaps during conversations like "mm" "uh" "and" "err", etc. It also includes discourse markers such as "well", "you know" and so on. Perhaps hedges can be classified into this category, too. According to Lakoff, hedges are words whose meaning implicitly involves fuzziness and whose job is to make things fuzzier or less fuzzy (1973). For example, "as far as I know" used when giving some information. All these elements are of no value in terms of information, but they are employed either to gain time in conversation, or to encode speakers' degree of commitment to the truth of what follows. Phatic communion refers to language used more for the purpose of establishing an atmosphere or maintaining social contact than for exchanging information or ideas. For examples, in speech, phatic communion includes informal comments on the weather or an enquiry about health at the beginning of a conversation or when passing someone in the street; and in writing, phatic communion includes the conventions for opening or closing a letter. As is clear to us, all those communication words are not aiming to exchange information but just to show closeness or friendliness.

Wei Junxuan(2002) discusses the relationship between redundancy and language communication. In this article, he analyzes the formation of redundancy and the factors affecting the degree of redundancy. According to him, people can use redundancy consciously to achieve expected communication goals. Therefore redundancy is divided into two types: redundancy in linguistic symbols and redundancy in communication. The former includes grammatical morphemes and semantic recurrence. But there is no detailed presentment of the latter type. The factors affecting redundancy include context, style, communication channel and ways, purposes and accepters. And there are some active functions of redundancy in communication: strengthening the ability of transmitted information for anti-interference; enhancing comprehensibility; emphasizing certain meanings; weakening certain meanings; canceling implicatures.

本章是对有关冗余的已有研究进行文献综述，列举在这一特殊领域的各种研究和成就。在这一领域，学者们从微观和宏观层面进行了大量的研究。不同的研究者对"冗余"持有不同的观点。他们有的从翻译的角度表达自己的观点，有的从修辞的角度给出自己的主张，有的把目光锁定在二语习得上。申农认为，根据信息论，冗余被认为是克服噪声的一种手段。美国著名学者奈达认为冗余反映了语言的可预测性。中国学者钱冠廉认为冗余的使用是由交际目的所驱动的，使用适当的冗余有助于实现交际目的。王红将冗余分为重复、迂回、填充语和寒暄语。对于冗余这一话题，许胜焕、桂世春等人也发表了他们对语言现象——冗余的看法，从字面上和实际上列举了大量的例子。

Chapter 3 A Working Definition of Redundancy and Its Manifestations

From the above analysis, we can see neither the micro nor the macro defining schemes are able to provide a full yet operable description of redundancy. None of them is free of perfection. Therefore it is necessary to give a working definition of this book before the in-depth discussion of the sorts and functions of redundancy.

3.1 Entropy, Information and Meaning

The concept of redundancy is first put forward in Information Theory and there are various comprehensions of it in many other fields, so when it is studied from a linguistic perspective and to propose a working definition, it is necessary to clarify some related concepts.

In Information Theory, entropy is a measure of the uncertainty associated with a random variable. The term by itself in this context usually refers to the Shannon entropy, which quantifies, in the sense of an expected value, the information contained in a message, usually in units such as bits. Equivalently, the Shannon entropy is a measure of the average information content one is missing when one does not know the value of the random variable. It represents an absolute limit on the best possible lossless compression of any communication and treats messages to be encoded as a sequence of independent and identically-distributed random variables. Shannon's source coding theorem shows that, in the limit, the average length of the shortest possible representation to encode the messages in a given alphabet is their entropy divided by the logarithm of the number of symbols in the target alphabet. Shannon & Weaver (1949) introduces the idea of the relative entropy: Hoo/Ho, in which the Hoo stands for the ratio of the actual entropy of a source, while the denominator Ho stands for the maximum entropy it could have while still restricted to the same symbols. Redundancy is the difference between the entropy of the ensemble of messages actually transmitted and the maximum entropy of the ensemble that the channel could transmit. So "1-Hoo/Ho" stands for the ratio of redundancy.

Redundancy in information theory is the number of bits used to transmit a message minus the number of bits of actual information in the message. It arises when there are more signals than necessary to distinguish a linguistic unit. Informally, it is the amount of wasted "space" used to transmit certain data. Data compression is a way to reduce or eliminate unwanted redundancy, while checksum is a way of adding desired redundancy for purposes of error detection when communicating over a noisy channel of limited capacity. It correlates in a statistically verifiable manner with the probability of occurrence of the particular element of information, that is, the more probable the occurrence of a particular sign, or the more frequently a particular expression is used, the less information value it has. Littlejohn defines redundancy as the sequence of letters in a word and the overall pattern of a sentence. He thinks the greater the uncertainty is, the more information there is (Littlejohn, 1992:315). Here, the information does not refer to meaning but only refers to the quantification of stimuli or signals. In this sense, each word is just a quantified stimulus and what information theorists concern is the probability of stimulus A being followed by stimulus B. Random strings letters like GHKIUT convey information instead of meaning because the information here is associated with how many choices being involved when we construct messages but those letters are totally unpredictable. Therefore, meaning only results from partial predictability. Message of complete uncertainty is just nonsense. Information and meaning are two different things in information theory. Weaver points out in his introduction to Shannon's paper:

The word information, in this theory, is used in a special sense that must not be confused with its ordinary usage. In particular information must not be confused with meaning. In fact, two messages, one of which is heavily loaded with meaning and the other of which is pure nonsense, can be exactly equivalent, from the present viewpoint, as regards information (Shannon & Weaver, 1949).

In this study, the term information is not used in that sense, because meaning and functions, rather than the quantification of stimuli or signals, are the main interest of the study. The meaning of message refers to what it says, whether relevant or irrelevant, truly or falsely, about another state of affairs, while the information a message carries refers to what it, among other things, relevantly and truly says about another state of affairs (Fred Dretske, 1998). So in this way, the term "information" is not used in the original sense of information theory, instead it could be understood as "facts told, heard or discovered about something or someone" (Hornby, 1997) or "knowledge of a specific event or situation". "To be communicative" and "to be informative" should also be distinguished. The former does not necessarily transmit new information, whereas the latter does. A phatic expression like "How are you doing?" is communicative but not informative, as there is no new information to the hearer. On the other hand, a highly informative expression like "kore-ha hon desu" is totally nonsense to a person who does not know anything about the Japanese language. In a word, redundancy cannot be simply regarded as being inversely related to efficiency.

3.2 A Working Definition for Redundancy

After conducting a systematic survey and making a clarification of the related concepts, let us give a tentative definition of redundancy in this book as follows: Redundancy refers to any linguistic unit that can be cancelled and simplified in a certain context. A linguistic unit is regarded as a redundant signal if the information it contains has already existed in other linguistic signals, or can be expressed in a briefer way, or irrelevant to the intended message.

In this definition, there are several defining elements of redundancy needing to be elaborated on.

3.2.1 Context

Context in linguistics is also called the environment of language—the environment in which the speech acts take place (Lv Xu, 2004). It is the core concept in pragmatics. To explain a linguistic phenomenon from pragmatic point of view, we must touch upon context. According to Leech (1983), pragmatics is concerned with how to use appropriate Linguistic means to perform a speech act and achieve an intended pragmatic effect (instead of linguistic meaning) in a given context. Of course, only the redundancy in a certain context can be called redundancy, otherwise, it is nearly impossible to define in sucha broad sense. First, let us have a general understanding of context. Context is so broad that different fields and different classes in one filed have different understanding. As for the connotation of it, the scholars at home and abroad have given all kinds of exposition. According to Malinowski (1944), there are three kinds of context: they are context of utterance, context of situation and context of culture. J. R. Firth (1957) divides context into linguistic context and situational context. M. A. K. Halliday (1973) concludes context as three parts: field, tenor and mode. Veschueren (2000) classifies context into communicative context and linguistic context. Although there are differences in all those perspectives and the terminologies they use are not the same, we can know the essential and the basic content of context from them. According to that, we generally recognize that two aspects are involved in context: linguistic context and extra-linguistic context. Linguistic context is the environment for language itself in which a linguistic units appear, which can be subdivided into phonetic and phonological context, grammatical context and text context. This book mainly discusses text context which mainly concerns the relationships between words, sentences and paragraphs in a text.

Extra-linguistic context is the social circumstances in which an event occurs, including the background knowledge, situational context and the mutual understanding of the interlocutors.

Compared with linguistic context, extra-linguistic context is so broad and variable that it is much more difficult to control and master. But in order to make a full understanding of a linguistic unit we must take both of them into consideration.

Context is dynamic and the meanings are changing for all levels of language units. Wood (1994) also points out "communication is a dynamic, systematic process in which meanings are created and reflected in humansinteraction with symbols". That is to say, context is the production in dynamic interaction between speakers and hearers in relation to what is/comes at that time and that place; it always changes with the proceeding of conversations. With the changing of context, the meanings of language units also differ from one to another as illustrated above. In a word, both context and the meaning of linguistic units are not stable; by contrary, they are in a state of change.

3.2.2 Linguistic unit

In the definition, linguistic units do not only refer to the lexical level but range from a word to a group of sentences. That is to say, redundancy can appear as a word, a clause, or even a sentence. For instance, redundancies in the following examples are respectively in lexical level, clause level and sentential level.

(1) You are *as young as* your faith, *as old as* your doubt; *as young as* your self-confidence, *as old as* your fear; *as young as* your hope, *as old as* your despair. (Unman)

(2) Yesterday, December 7, 1941-*a date which will live in infamy*-the United States of American was suddenly and deliberately attacked by navel and air forces of the Empire of Japan. (Franklin)

(3) *Those kids were getting in all right*, with busted heads and bleeding faces-those kids, *were getting it all right*. (Griffith)

3.2.3 Existing information

Existing information refers to the information which has been transmitted by the preceding signals. We also can name it "old information". For instance:

(4) All of our people have the same goals, *the same objective*. (Malcolm)

3.2.4 Expressions in a briefer way

Sometimes we use a roundabout way to express our minds, but in fact we can say it in a much simpler way or use fewer words. For example:

(5) Such being the case, *we have no choice but to* request you to amend relative contract terms.

This sentence can be expressed in a briefer way: we request you to amend relative contract terms for this reason. However, the pragmatic function is with great disparity: the latter pattern seems impolite and unnatural in normal business relationship.

3.2.5 Irrelevant message

Some units are irrelevant to the intended message and transmit no information such as the verbal fillers. Here, for instance, the words "oh", "ah" and "why" and the phrase "you know" in the following example are irrelevant messages:

(6) "*Oh*, *ah*, *why*—give you fair warning—look out, *you know*—that's all," said the mustachio-twiddler. (Thackeray)

From the elaboration, the development and features of this definition can be seen as follows:

1. Circular definitions such as "redundancy is the state of being redundant" can be avoided.

2. It doesn't use any words like "superfluous" that will give people a negative association.

3. This definition takes context into consideration.

4. The study of redundancy in this book is in a macro-perspective.

In distinguishing redundancy, we should not confuse it with vagueness and ambiguity. The word "Vague" means not clearly expressed or not exact. If a word or phrase is said to be vague, that means it provides less information and its meaning is not clear in the given context. Let us take a simple example, if a speaker says, "I have something to do tomorrow", we could not know what is meant by "something", for the word "something" can be referred to anything. Ambiguity means an expression presents more than one meaning in a certain context. For instance, "Look at those pretty little girls' dresses" is ambiguous, because it is not clear whether the girls or the dresses are "pretty". By "ambiguity", we do not know which of the two specific meaning is intended. As for redundancy, it provides no (new) information at least literally.

3.3 The Manifestations of Redundancy

The manifestations of redundancy are diversified in nature because there are too many aspects of redundancy that can be used as the criteria for categorization. According to the study interest, redundancy can be classified into lexical, clausal, sentential, and discoursal redundancy in the linguistic level.

Eugene A. Nida, the most famous translation theorists, should be definitely mentioned when it comes to the manifestation of redundancy. This famous linguist contributes a lot to the theory of communicative translation. When he talks about communication, he takes redundancy into consideration.

By saying that language incorporate a great deal of redundancy into their structures, we simply say that language reflects a good deal of predictability. It is rather easily seen if we experiment with leaving out letters from words. For example, in the following partially written words the reader can usually supply the missing letters with considerable facility:

C__ Y__ s_m__d_ t__s?

It dose not take much puzzling with this series to recognize that the intended sentence is "Can you see me do this?" (Nida, 1963).

Nida (1963) believes that redundancy is calculated as a left-to-right procedure; that is to say, the predictability of a following form is calculated upon the extent to which preceding forms determine its probability of occurrence. Thus if a particular term occurs after a series of delimiting or qualifying expressions, it is much more redundant than if it occurs first. For example, in the phrase *all these destitute*, *ragged X*, the final form X can be filled only with some such words as *people*, *persons*, *waifs*, *orphans*; it cannot include such words as *animals*, *bushes*, *stones*, *squares*, *triangles*, or *happenings*. But if we use the expression *these X*, *who were destitute and ragged*, it is much more difficult to predict what X will be if we only have the preceding *these*. In actual speech, however, as well as in the understanding of written materials, people do not decode merely from left to right. Rather, they take in what might be called meaningful mouthfuls and actually determine the meaning by two-directional decoding, so that redundancy must be calculated both lineally and structurally. Of course, if the preceding elements give almost all the requested information, the last of the phrase is highly redundant.

Moreover, some of the clues to the proper item in the first of a phrase may be supplied only at considerable length, e. g. *These X, who came to visit us last week, insisted that they be paid.*

As for the manifestation of redundancy, another Chinese scholar, Qian Guanlian (1997) believes that every speaker has the intention to produce certain communicative effects when speaking; therefore, communication is a goal-oriented activity, during which various different types of goals interact. The speaker, in order to achieve his ultimate goal, has to employ all kinds of effective communicational means, including the Cooperative Principle. However, sometimes in language practice, this principle may be violated, for successful communication is not always influenced by whether the speaker is cooperative or not, but only motivated by the goal of communication. Redundancy can help achieve communicational goals if it is used appropriately.

Additionally, Xu Shenghuan (1984) from China divides the redundancy into two kinds: reiteration and implication. The former means the recurrence of the same linguistic unit, synonym unit, similarity unit and co-reference unit. And the latter means the information in one expression unit which can be inferred from another one. Gillette & Wit (1998) classify linguistic redundancy into what they call "contextual redundancy" and "grammatical redundancy". Conversely, Darwish (1995) divides redundancy into intra-cultural and inter-cultural redundancy in terms of culture-sensitive nature of redundancy. Some language phenomenon in one culture is indispensable but redundant in different cultures. For instance, in Japanese, the social hierarchy is embedded in language itself. The linguistic signals that denote the rank, status and social distance are not redundant in Japanese, but are redundant in other languages with different cultures. To talk about the manifestation, Wang

Hong (2000) classifies redundancy into four types from the point view of pragmatics: repetition, circumlocution, verbal fillers and phatic communication. Repetition refers to doing, saying or writing the same thing more than once. The recurrence of processes, structures, elements and motifs are fundamental to communication in general and to language in particular. Such repetition occurs at all levels, starting with rhythm. Repetition further includes repetition of form and repetition of meaning. Let us have a look of the following examples. In Example (1), the same word "any" is repeated for five times, while in Example (2) and (3), "pomp" and "pageantry", "pick" and "choose" are different words, but they express the similar meaning. Both of them belong to redundancy.

1) *Any* right that is available to *any* single man should be available to *any* woman *any*where in the world at *any* time.

2) The marriage of Prince Charles and Princess Diana, launched amidst *pomp and pageantry* 15 years ago, proved calamitous.

3) She likes to *pick and choose*.

Circumlocution, also called periphrasis, in rhetoric, is a wordy and indirect way of saying something. In other words, circumlocution refers to the use of many words where fewer would do, so it is regarded as a kind of redundancy. Such usage is often obscure, officious, pompous,

authoritarian and intimidating. For instances,

4) negative patient care outcome (death).

5) the husband of your father's sister (your uncle).

Verbal filler is an inclusive term here. It includes those meaningless sounds used to fill the gaps during conversations like *mm*, *uh*, and *err*, etc.

It also includes discourse markers like *well*, *you know* and others. Perhaps hedges can be classified into this category, too. According to Lakoff, hedges are words whose meaning implicitly involves fuzziness and whose job is to make things fuzzier or less fuzzy (1973), for example, *as far as I know* used when giving some information. All these elements are of no value in terms of information, but they are employed either to gain time in conversation, or to encode speakers' degree of commitment to the truth of what follows. Phatic communion refers to language used more for the purpose of establishing an atmosphere or maintaining social contact than for exchanging information or ideas. For examples, in speech, phatic communion includes informal comments on the weather (Example 6) or an enquiry about health at the beginning of a conversation or when passing someone in the street (Example 7); and in writing, phatic communion includes the conventions for opening or closing a letter (Example 8). As is clear to us, all these examples are not aiming to exchange information. They are used just to show closeness or friendliness.

6) Nice day again, isn't it?

7) How's it going?

Leg better?

8) All the best.

Yours faithfully

The four kinds of redundancy mentioned above are often found in language practice and all of them have been accepted by language users. However, it should be acknowledged that in language there also exists unacceptable redundancy, for instances, *walk home on foot*, *black dog in color* and *in my opinion*, *I think*... Such redundancy usually results from lack of language knowledge or misuse of language. Since the topic of this book is the positive functions of redundancy, unacceptable redundancy is not within the scope of our discussion.

According to Information Theory, redundancy is a means of combating noise. Nida thinks that redundancy reflects predictability in language. Qian Guanlian begins to lay emphasis on the value of redundancy. Wang Hong classifies redundancy into four types. Taking all these scholars' opinions into consideration, we hold that appropriate use of redundancy can play a positive role in language practice, so redundancy is a way to achieve different communicative effects. In the next chapter of this book we will discuss these positive functions of redundancy in detail.

Based on the above discussion, I try to provide an overall review of redundancy's characteristics, which can be briefly concluded as two types: redundancy in structure and redundancy in meaning.

3.3.1 Redundancy in structure

Structural redundancy means the redundant element can be seen in linguistic units ranging from word level to sentence level. It includes repetition and discourse markers.

Repetition

Repetition refers to doing, saying or writing the same thing more than once. Here repetition refers to rhetorical repetition which is one of the most often used devices in rhetoric. Generally speaking, it can be divided into immediate repetition and intermittent repetition. (Feng Cuihua, 2005)

A. Immediate Repetition

The repeating of linguistic units in close juxtaposition is the simplest, and the most common kind of repetition. The number of times a word, phrase or even a sentence is repeated may vary from two to any required number.

(1) Lady Macbeth: *To bed, to bed*; there's a knocking at the gate. *Come, come, come, come*, give me your hand. What's done cannot be undone. *To bed, to bed, to bed*. (Shakespeare: *Macbeth*)

(2) When I had waited a long time, very patiently, without hearing him lie down, I resolved to open a little—a very, very little crevice in the lantern. So I opened it—you cannot imagine how *stealthily, stealthily*—until, at length, a simple dim ray, like the thread of the spider, shot from out the crevice and fell full upon the vulture eye. (Allan Poe: *The Tell-Tale Heart*)

(3) "I gave it to her, I gave it to her," Ameba said. (Thackeray: *Vanity Fair*)

B. Intermittent Repetition

Intermittent repetition is the most widely used form of repetition, in which the linguistic units repeated are separated from each other by syntactic elements of varying length. It can be further divided into seven types: anaphora, epistrophe, symploce, epidiplosis, anadiplosis, antistrophe and tautology.

Anaphora is the repeating of a linguistic unit in initial or front position of successive clauses, sentences, stanzas or paragraphs. The usual pattern of it is(a...) (a...), for examples,

(4) The stories of past courage can define that ingredient-*they can* teach, *they can* offer hope, *they can* provide inspiration. (Kennedy: *Courage*)

(5) Young men are fitter to invent, *than to* judge; *fitter for* execution, *than for* counsel; and *fitter for* new projects, *than for* settled business. (Bacon: *Of Youth and Age*)

(6) "*I'm not afraid to die*... *I'm not afraid to* live. *I'm not afraid to*

fail. *I' m not afraid to* succeed. *I' m not afraid to* fall in love. *I' m not afraid to* be alone. I' m just afraid I might have to stop talking about myself five minutes." (Friedman: *When the Cat' s Away*)

Epistrophe, opposite of anaphora, refers to ending successive clauses, sentences, stanzas or paragraphs with the same linguistic unit. The usual pattern is(... a) (... a) ,for instances.

(7) When I was a child, I spoke *as a child*, I understood *as a child*, I thought *as a child*. (I Corithians 13.11)

(8) To be *alive*, to be man *alive*, to be whole man *alive*: that is the point. (Lawrence: *Phoenix*)

(9) "... it' s their wealth and security that makes everything *possible*, makes your art *possible*, makes literature science, even religion *possible*..." (Galsworthy: *the Man of Poverty*)

Symploce is the use of lexical anaphora and epistrophe in the same line or stanza, in the same clause or statement. That means the beginning and the end of the next sentence is the same with the beginning and the end of the last sentence. This kind of repetition often takes the pattern (a... b) (a... b), for examples.

(10)*Against* yourself you *are calling him*, *against* the laws you *are calling him*, *against* the democratic *you are calling him*.

(11) I thought he *was dumb*, I said he *was dumb*, Yet I' ve heard him cry. (Lawrence: *Tortoise Shout*)

Epidiplosis refers to the repetition of the same linguistic unit after the intervening syntactic units. More specifically, the initial and the ending parts are the same. This device repeats a sentence or a part of a sentence at both the begging and end of long sentences, stanzas or paragraphs. The pattern is

(a. . . a),for examples,

(12)*Blood* will have *blood*.

(13)*Waiting for the end*, *boys*, *waiting for the end*. Not a chance of blend, boys, things have got to tend. Think of those who vend, boys, think of how we wend, *Waiting for the end*, *boys*, *waiting for the end*. (Empson: *Just a Smack at Auden*)

In anadiplosis, the last linguistic units of the previous phrase, clause or sentence becomes the first parts of the next. In this device a word in the end position in a line or sentence is repeated in initial position in the line following. The pattern is(. . . a) (a. . .),for instancse.

(14)"Now, what I want is, *facts*. Teach these boys and girls nothing but *facts*. *Facts* alone are wanted in life."(Dickens: *Hard Times*)

(15) The secret of modern decorating is to apply some thing that looks like something else. There are plastic coverings that look like *cloth*, *cloth* coverings that look like *tile*, *tile* coverings that look like *metal*, *metal* covering that look like *wood*, and *wood* coverings that look like plastic. And the vice verse. (Williamson: *Wall Covering*)

In antistrophe, the repeated parts change their position, that's to say the second part is an inverted parallel of the first. It usually takes the pattern (a. . . b) (b. . . a),for examples.

(16)*Eat* to *live*, and not *live* to *eat*. (Franklin: *Poor Richard's Almanac*)

(17) It was the same everywhere *crime* and *betrayal*, *betrayal* and *crime*. (Jack London)

Tautology, also called ploce (Feng Cuihua, 2005) repeats a word to bring out emphatically its literal meaning. It is more limited in application and generally regarded as needless repetition of the same sense, because the words carry no new information Literally. For instances:

(18) *Children* are *children*.

(19) "They have *egg whites colored yellow and frozen*-and they tasted like *egg whites colored yellow and frozen*," he says. (Newsweek, Apr. 6, 1992)

Discourse markers

Discourse markers are an inclusive term here. It includes those meaningless sounds used to fill the gaps during conversations like "mm" "uh" and "err", etc. It also includes words like "well" "you know" "I mean", and "of course" which serve as structuring units instead of content words or phrases. Although these signals have not occurred before in the context and should be counted as new information according to the information theory, they still belong to redundancy because they contain no information and can be totally cancelled. It has been proved that their function in communication is pragmatic rather than semantic. Holker (1998) points out that there are four basic features of discourse markers: (1) They don't affect the true condition of the discourse; (2) they don't add prepositional content to the talking; (3) they are related to the discourse context but not the situation that being talked; (4) they have emotional and expressive function but no referential, denotative and cognitive function. The italic words or phrase in the following examples are discourse markers:

(20) Every new step, *you see*, is a trial and you have to prove that you're capable of going beyond that.

(21) And most of it, *as you know*, or perhaps you don't, is rooted in scientific fact.

(22) Babylon 5 is a series set in the future about 250-some-odd years, aboard a space station which is about 5 miles long, and serves as a port of call, or a way station, *if you will*, similar to Venice, or other parts of Europe during the 14 th century.

3.3.2 Redundancy in meaning

Redundancy in meaning refers to the redundant symbols which are not obviously presented in the form but in the meaning. It can be divided into circumlocution and implication.

Circumlocution

Circumlocution, which in another term is called periphrasis, circumduction, circumvolution, periphrase or orambage in rhetoric, is a roundabout figure of speech or a wordy and indirect way of saying something. In its most basic form, circumlocution is using many words such as "a tool used for cutting things such as paper and hair" to describe something simple ("scissors"). In other words, circumlocution refers to the use of many words where fewer would do, so it is regarded as a kind of redundancy. For examples:

(23) A: I was wondering if we could meet again on the 24 th.

B: As a matter of fact, I'm afraid that might be a bit difficult as I have to contact one or two colleagues who I do know are out of the country at the moment. Perhaps we could give a word with them. Quite important that I have a word with them. Wouldn't the following Thursday, the 31 st, be better?

In fact, A wants to say "I want to meet you on the 24 th", and B just want to express "that's not suitable. Let's make it on the 31 st". Therefore, the speeches of A and B are redundant for their roundabout way of expression.

(24) A: Did you win the game?

B: Well, in the first round, I didn't win; in the second round, he didn't lose; in the third round, I wanted a draw, but he didn't agree.

Obviously, we all know the meaning of B's speaking and of course he can simply say he lost all the three rounds, but he used an indirect way to keep his face or to create a sense of humor.

Implication

To some degree, implication is also a kind of repetition; it is the repetition of the meaning rather than the linguistic symbols. In implication, the information contained in the latter symbols has already existed in the former ones. This kind of repetition can be produced through modifiers, synonym and homoionym.

In order to emphasize the meaning or express a strong feeling, we often adopt some modifiers to a noun with the former implicitly containing some features of the latter, e. g.

Chinese phrase "胜利的凯歌" means a song for victory, but "凯" in Chinese contains the Chinese meaning of victory, so here the adjective and the noun express the same meaning, that is to say the phrase is repetitive in the information of winning. The situation is the same with the Chinese phrase "悬殊很大". In Chinese, "悬殊" means the disparity between two things is great, while "很大" also means very big or large. So this adverb is the repetition of the noun and it produces the redundancy. Let us look at some examples in English:

a silly fool: we all know fool is a person who is unwise and considered as silly, therefore silly and fool are mutual repetition in meaning and here comes redundancy.

an unexpected surprise: certainly the surprise is out of expectation. So the adjective also belongs to the redundant element. The modifiers in the above examples do not add new information to the add it modifies, therefore they are redundant in the meaning.

Synonym refers to a word having the same or similar meaning as another word. It can use repetition of an idea several times in different words to produce implication. That is also called commoratio in rhetoric. A good example of it is John Cleese used synonyms beyond the point of absurdity in the *Dead Parrot Sketch*:

He's passed on! This parrot is no more! He has ceased to be! He's expired and gone to meet his maker! He's a stiff! Bereft of life, he rests in peace! If you hadn't nailed him to the perch he'd be pushing up the daisies! His metabolic processes are now history! He's off the twig! He's kicked the bucket; he's shuffled off his mortal coil, run down the curtain and joined thebleedin' choir invisible! THIS IS AN EX-PARROT!

In his description, eight different phrases are used to express the same meaning of death.

Therefore, at the beginning of the main body of this book, it is necessary to clarify what redundancy exactly is. We can see that the definitions from the above are somewhat different in version, but the essence of redundancy is the same: more information than is needed. In communication, there is a minimum amount of information that can guarantee reasonable understanding. While in reality, for various purposes, information beyond the minimum amount is often provided, and this exceeding part of information is regarded as redundancy. In summary, through this chapter we can see different manifestations of redundancy and after a full-scale scanning, we have a working definition of redundancy, which is hopefully a foundation for the following analysis of this book.

本章综合了国内外学者的研究成果,试图给出一个可行的冗余的定义,并探讨冗余的表现形式。"语言冗余"是一种语言现象,要求以自然语言为研究对象,主要涉及语境和语言单位、现有信息和无关信息等多个方面。语言的冗余形式包括结构上的冗余和意义上的冗余。

Chapter 4
Pragmatic Functions of Redundancy

Countless examples show that various forms of redundancy are not nonsense at all. On the contrary, they often play a very important role in successful communication.

Let us take "well" for example. ① It appears frequently in conversation, although it does not carry any concrete meaning itself. Its usages can be illustrated as follows:

Well can serve as a means of mitigation of face threatening acts, politely expressing disagreement or refusal. For example,

(1) A: Can I see them?

B: *Well*, I'm not allowed to do that.

If a speaker does not know what to say or hesitates about what to say, he often uses *well* to fill the pause. For example,

(2) A: How much are you selling for your car?

B: *Well*, how about 4,000 dollars?

---

① The examples of "well" are quoted from Svartvik, J. *Well in Conversation*

Speakers may employ *well* as an insufficiency marker when information is not adequately supplied. For instance, in Example (3) speaker B actually omits *Korea is a good place for learning English* and says *well* instead.

(3) A: The man speaks extremely good English.

B: *Well*, he comes from Korea.

Well can also be used to do self-repair when a speaker realizes there is something wrong in his words. For example,

(4) A: What did you do?

B: We walked along in silence for a bit, *well*, not really silence because she was bumming.

Besides, *well* may act as a reinforcement marker to enhance communicative effects. For instance,

(5) A: He's very busy at the moment.

B: Yes, *well*, he's always frantically busy.

When a speaker wants to go back to an earlier topic or introduce a new start, he can use *well*, too, as in Example (6):

(6) If they wanted people around to talk to, then I would be very happy to stay. We have arranged for you to stay. *Well*, let's take the interview first.

Semantically *well* does not contain any meaning. Conversation can still go on smoothly if it is omitted, but from the above examples we can see that it can make expressions more natural and graceful, and convey humans feelings and thoughts more effectively.

In a word, redundancy has its own unique functions and vitality. In language practice, it is true that redundancy is usually employed intentionally to achieve certain kinds of pragmatic effects. In the following part of this chapter, we will discuss the pragmatic functions of redundancy in detail.

4.1 Functions of Redundancy in Terms of the Cooperative Principle

Theoretically, the Cooperative Principle can help explain redundancy. Redundancy is closely related to the Cooperative Principle mainly in two ways, that is redundancy may either help to follow the Cooperative Principle (more exactly, to follow the Quantity Maxim), or help to flout the Cooperative Principle, resulting in implicatures. Following or flouting the Cooperative Principle in one way or another, redundancy gives a deeper and more subjective meaning of the words or expressions and takes the reader or hearer beyond the literal meaning.

4.1.1 A Brief Review of the Cooperative Principle

H. P. Grice is a philosopher who has concerned himself with philosophical issues in language use. One of his major contributions is his concept of the Cooperative Principle and four associated maxims, proposed to account for the structure of conversation. These ideas were developed in *Logic and Conversation* (1975). Simply, Grice suggests a principle and maxims which guide speakers and hearers in carrying out a successful conversation. According to Grice, when the principle or any of the maxims is flouted, what is called *conversational implicatures* will occur, which is a special kind of meaning. This idea of implicature has become a key concept in pragmatic analysis.

In order to explain further the cooperative principle, abbreviated as CP, Grice borrows from the German philosopher Immanuel Kant four categories: quantity, quality, relation and manner. That is, the CP is specified from these four categories, and the content of each category is known as maxim.

The category of Quantity, concerned with the quantity of information to be provided, has two maxims:

Maxim 1: Make your contribution as informative as is required (for the current purposes of the exchange).

Maxim 2: Do not make your contribution more informative than is required.

In the category of Quality there is a super maxim:

Try to make your contribution the one that is true.

and two specific maxims:

Maxim 1: Do not say what you believe to be false.

Maxim 2: Do not say that for which you lack adequate evidence.

The category of Relation has a single maxim *Be relevant*. "Though the maxim itself is terse, its formulation conceals a number of problems that exercise me a good deal: questions about what different kinds and focuses of relevance there may be, how these shift in the course of a talk exchange, how to allow for the fact that subjects of conversation are legitimately changed, and so on." (Grice, 1975)

As for the category of Manner, it is different from others. According to Grice, this category doesn't relate "to what is said but rather, to how what is said is to be said." (Grice, 1975) There is also a super maxim *Be perspicuous*, and the specific maxims are:

Maxim 1: Avoid obscurity of expression.

Maxim 2: Avoid ambiguity.

Maxim 3: Be brief (avoid unnecessary prolixity).

Maxim 4: Be orderly.

This theory not only reveals the nature of successful communication, but also serves as a powerful explanation of a lot of incoherent and unnatural linguistic phemomena.

4.1.2 Cooperative Functions of Redundancy

One way that CP is relevant to redundancy is that redundancy may enable speakers to follow the Cooperative Principle. In this respect, hedges are very good examples. As far as information is concerned, hedges do not have much value, so we regard them as redundancy; however, the uses of hedges do help speakers to be more cooperative. In order to make it clearer, let us to have a look of the way that hedges help speakers comply to the four maxims one by one.

The importance of the Maxim of Quality for cooperative interaction in English may be best measured by the number of expressions we use to indicate that what we're saying may not be totally accurate. The initial phrases in (7a-c) and the final phrase in (7d) are notes to the listener regarding the accuracy of the main statcment. The conversational context for the examples might be a recent rumor involving a couple known to the speakers.

(7) a. *As far as I know*, they're married.

b. I *may be* mistaken, but I thought I saw a wedding ring on her finger.

c. *I'm not sure if* this is right, but I heard it was a secret ceremony in Hawaii.

d. He couldn't live without her, *I guess*.

Cautious notes or hedges can also be used to show that the speaker is conscious of the Maxim of Quantity, as in the initial phrases in (8a-c), produced in the course of a speaker's account of her recent vacation.

(8) a. *As you probably know*, I am terrified of bugs.

b. So, *to cut a long story short*, we grabbed our stuff and ran.

c. *I won't bother you with all the details*, but it was an exciting trip.

Markers tied to the expectation of relevance (from the Maxim of Relation) can be found in the middle of a conversation when speakers say things like *Oh*, *by the way* and go on to mention some potentially unconcerned information during a conversation. Speakers also seem to use expressions like *anyway* or *well, anyway* to indicate that they may have drifted into a discussion of some possibly non-relevant material and want to stop. Some expressions which may act as hedges on the expectation of relevance are shown as the initial phrases in (9a-c), from an office meeting.

(9) a. *I don't know if this is important*, but some of the files are missing.

b. *This may sound like a dumb question*, but whose handwriting is this?

c. *Not to change the subject*, but is this related to the budget?

The awareness of the Maxim of Manner may also lead speakers to produce hedges of the type shown in the initial phrases in (10a-c), heard during an account of a crash.

(10) a. This may be a bit confused, but I remember being in a car.

b. I'm not sure if this makes sense, but the car had no lights.

c. I don't know if this is clear at all, but I think the other car was reversing.

All of these examples of hedges indicate that the speakers are not only aware of the maxims, but also want to show that they are trying to observe the maxins by the employment of redundancy. Perhaps the employment of redundancy also reveals the speakers' concern that their listeners judge them to be cooperative conversational partners.

4.2 Functions of Redundancy in Terms of Implicature

The other way in which CP is of interest for the study of redundancy is that, to a great extent, redundancy means violation of maxims, especially the Maxim of Quantity and the Maxim of Relation. Grice explains that in conversations, speakers very often break rather than follow the maxims (1975). When they do this, specific effects are created on hearers, for which Grice gives the term implicatures. According to the core idea of Relevance Theory, communication is an ostensive-inferential process, during which the communicator produces stimuli to the audience to make manifestation for a set of assumptions. With those assumptions in certain context, the audience will find out the optimal relevant one and finally get the implicated meaning of the communicator. Discourse markers, one of the manifestations of redundancy, are a typical kind of such stimuli that can direct hearers to find out the optimal relevant assumptions and thus decrease the effort during the inferential process.

4.2.1 Implicature and Relevance Theory

Relevance Theory is developed from Grice's maxims by Sperber & Wilson (1986), who also concern implicature but the interpretation is quite different. They reduce all Gricean maxims to a single all-compassing cognitive principle: the principle of relevance, which views communication as essentially the recognition of the speaker's intention by the audience. In Sperber and Wilson's opinion, to get the right meaning of natural language, we should look for the relevance in context and then comprehend through inference. So they put forward an ostensive-inferential communication model. Inferential communication and ostentation are the same thing seen from two different angles. To speakers, it is ostentation, showing, or making manifest of his informative intention; while to hearers, it is inference, inferring from the evidence presenting the speaker's intentions. There are two terms in this theory to distinguish speaker's literal meaning and intentions—explicature and implicature. The latter is based on the former and gained by inference in context. During the process of inference, hearers make a set of assumptions through the stimulus produced by speakers, and then find out the optimal relevance between the immediate context and the information.

4.2.2 Analysis for Implicature of Redundancy in Terms of Relevance Theory

Now, let us take discourse markers, one kind of redundancy, as an example to interpret redundancy in terms of Relevance Theory. Blakemore (1987, 1988, and 1992) and other scholars have done specific research on discourse markers with Relevance Theory. According to the result, discourse markers neither affect the truth condition of the utterance nor add proposition content. Since discourse markers have nothing to do with the meaning of the expression and are redundant elements, why do speakers often use them in discourses? The most effective and tentative answer is given by Blakemore. She points out that the aim for using discourse markers is to decrease the effort in comprehension of hearers at maximum degree; and the function of them is to demonstrate the feature and effect of context, which will help hearers make necessary assumptions with relatively less effort. That is to say, discourse markers can reduce the effort when we look for the optimal relevance between the context and the information because they play a role of instruction, which can exclude some impossible or irrelevant assumptions and direct the hearers to choose the optimal assumption and then get the only right understanding of the utterance. Generally speaking, in communication, on the one hand, a speaker who intends his utterance to be interpreted in a particular way must expect the hearer to be able to supply a context which allows that interpretation to be recovered without too much effort to find the relevance. On the other hand, a hearer who wishes to draw the intended implication must construct his context and find out the most related assumption on the basis of the proposition expressed by the speaker. In the Principle of Relevance, by producing an utterance, a speaker always constrains the hearer's contextual assumptions, thus ensures the hearer to reach the intended goal at minimal processing cost. This licenses the hearer to believe that the least costly interpretation is the one the speaker intends. Therefore, in order to make the optimal assumption much easier to gain for the hearer, the speaker can use discourse markers to give instruction and restrict the interpretation process, which will lead the hearer to get the right meaning; at the same time, the hearer is sure what the speaker said must be relevant to his intention and tries to find some clues and hints for the implicature through the discourse markers. On normal occasions, the more direct and explicit an utterance is, the more easily the utterance yields the expected contextual effect, and the tighter the hearer's interpretation is constrained.

M. Goodable once talked about *um* in Language of meeting:

Obviously understanding *um*s will help in any negotiation with an Anglo-Saxon; using *um*s may help you to make your meaning clearer, and encourage acceptance of your conditions. In addition, when you reply to a question, *ums* make it seem as if you had not foreseen the question, which in turn puts the person asking at ease. If you reply in a firm, direct way, it can appear premeditated and appear as a challenge, promoting the other party to go on the defensive. You may have wanted to show your decisiveness, but the result may be attack!

Jan Svartvik (1980) commented on well in conversation: "... if someone says 'four sheeps' or 'she goed' in English, almost all the native people can tell the grammar errors. But if someone omitted *well* in conversation, he or she will give others an impression of rude, impolite and peremptoriness. No one would point out the inappropriateness. Therefore, we can see that not using or misusing the discourse markers like 'well' in communication is a mistake more serious than that of some grammar errors." Those are the comments for functions of discourse markers. Now, this book will explain discourse markers in terms of Relevance Theory and take some examples in *Vanity Fair* to show how they help both speakers to produce implicatures and hearers to interpret the intended meaning.

(11) "I cannot, certainly," she said, "find fault with Miss Sharp's conduct, *except* to me; and must allow that her talents and accomplishments are of a high order. As far as head goes, at least, she does credit to the educational system pursued at my establishment."

That was the recommendation from Miss Pinkerton to Sir Pitt Crawley's family for Rebecca as a governess. We all know Miss Pinkerton and Rebecca hate each other, and the relationship between them was very bad. Certainly the former would not speak high of the latter. But considering the result, she could not say directly and too much about her true feeling towards Rebecca, so she chose two discourse markers "except" and "at least" to indicate that she did not like the referee in some way and what worth her recommendation was only the education in her school.

(12) "I've come home *FOR GOOD*, you know; and this is my friend,

Miss Sharp, whom you have heard me mention."

Before Rebecca entered upon her duties as governess in a private family, Ameba invited her friend to pass a week with her at home. When she saw her brother Joseph, she said she would come home for good. Here "for good" was ambiguous but certainly was not undersigned. In order to make her brother aware what was her "for good", she used "you know" to imply and then introduced Rebecca to him. From his escape later (for his shyness), we know, thanks for the hints, he got the impicature of the "good" then.

(13) "By Gad, Miss Sharp, I wouldn't hurt you for the world."

"No," said she, "I KNOW you wouldn't...

When Joseph appeared after several days' panic, his family mentioned the trick he played on Rebecca and laughed again. Rebecca deliberately criticized him for his evil. Of course, he denied it. Facing the like-vow-answer, she was very pleased and agreed with him. But she didn't just say "no, you wouldn't" but added "I know", which obviously was intended to show her feeling to him and implied that she would let him treat her well in future. With the hints of Rebecca's language and behavior, Joseph got the intended meaning and his heart thumped as the author described.

(14) "Seems be hanged, Dobbin," his junior interrupted him. "I am under obligations to you, I know it, a d-d deal too well too; but I won't be always sermonized by you because you're five years my senior..."

Seeing the attitude of George to Ameba, Dobbin could not stand it and quarreled with him. He hoped George could care about Ameba and treat her better. But George refused to listen and asked Dobbin not to interfere his matter so much. First he committed his obligation he owned to Dobbin and used the word "too" to emphasize. In common sense, all that he committed should lead to a compromise, to our surprise, he used the "but" to turn the point and reveal his real thoughts that he was unwilling to be always under the control. Also the reason for his dissatisfaction was introduced by the word "because". Apparently, that reason was far enough for being sermonized. What these words implied there was to point out Dobbin's officious manner towards other's business.

(15) "Well, suppose he is fond of me. I know he is, and the others too. You don't think I am afraid of him, Captain Crawley? You don't suppose I can't defend my own honor." said the little woman, looking as stately as a queen.

"Oh, ah, why—give you fair warning—look out, you know—that's all." said the mustachio-twiddler.

To the inquiry of the attitude towards his father's attachment from Rawdon, Rebecca turned back with "well", which was used to indicate she had something to say. And in her statement, actually she had known about it and the word "too" implied that not only his father but also others liked her either. But she would not accept them as she refuted. Not having expected Bush firm answers that Rawdon felt embarrassed and could not give a proper reply for his inquiry immediately, so he used three hesitation fillers to suggest he would give some reasons. And in order to conceal his real purpose, he used "you know" to remind Rebecca he just wanted to give her a warning.

(16) "But it's not about marriage that I came to speak—that is that marriage—that is—no, I mean—my dear Miss Osborne, it's about our dear friend George." Dobbin said.

Without permission of his father, Osborne got married with Ameba, which caused the whole family very angry and the relationship nearly broken up. At this time, both Dobbin and Osborne received the order to go abroad for war. After their leaving, Ameba would be along. In order to let Osborne's family accept Ameba, Dobbin went to Osborne's home. He thought it might be easier to have the ladies on his side. Therefore, he began his persuasion with Miss Osborne, who loved him very much and hoped he could marry her. When Dobbin talked with her about the marriage, she mistakenly thought that's the prelude for his proposal to her. Recognizing that, Dobbin turned the topic with "but" at once to call her attention and implied what he wanted to say was something else. But because he was so nervous that he couldn't organize his words well; at last, he used "I mean" to turn to his real point. And finally, Miss Osborne got the right comprehension of the aim for his coming.

So in linguistic communication, when there are discourse markers like "except" "at least" "I know" "you know" "too" "well" "because" "after all" "any way" and "but" we can follow the speaker's instructions and go on to discover his intended implicatures. Therefore, from the above examples we can see discourse markers are successfully employed by the hearer since they are facilitative for understanding.

4.2.3 Implicature and Indirect Speech Acts

Circumlocution is one of the manifestations of redundancy which uses many words to say something that could be said in fewer words. In other sense, it is a roundabout and indirect way of saying, which can help people to be polite and convey more than what is said. Therefore it can be explained in terms of Indirect Speech Act. Let us have a clarification of what is the relationship between implicature and indirect speech acts.

As for the concept of indirect speech acts, there have been many studies and opinions about it. It was first put forward by American philosopher J. Searle and developed from J. L. Austin's Speech Act Theory, which holds that people use language to perform acts. According to this theory, all the speech acts can be divided into direct and indirect speech acts. If a person achieves the communication goals directly through literal meaning, it is the direct speech act; while a person puts some extra meaning in the utterance, then it is the indirect speech act.

Searle (1975) develops this concept and points out that indirect speech acts are "cases in which one illocutionary acts is performed indirectly by way of performing another." (1975) He thinks that in a certain context, if only there is no difference between the literal meaning and the intended meaning of words and sentences, it is direct speech acts; otherwise, if the speaker wants to use the words to express some other meanings beyond the letters, it is indirect speech act. Leech (1983) points out, when speakers utter a sentence to convey the literal meaning, they also express an extra meaning, the difference between the sentence meaning and the utterance meaning is the indirect speech act. He Zhaoxiong (1989) thinks the indirectness of speech is brought by the form and the function of linguistic symbols. He also says, we can explain indirect speech acts from the relation between literal meaning and utterance meaning: when there is difference between the two meanings, the use of language is indirect speech acts. Sun Yu (1994) concludes that the shared characteristic of indirect speech acts is the disparity between sentence meaning and utterance meaning. From those interpretations, we can get the essential characteristics of indirect speech acts: there is difference between literal meaning and underline meaning. As we stated at the beginning of this chapter, those differences are in fact the implicatures produced by speakers or writers.

4.2.4 Implicature of Redundancy in Terms of Indirect Speech Acts

From the above clarification, we know circumlocution gets the essential characteristics of indirect speech acts and it is one kind of them. Now, let us take some examples from *Vanity Fair* to see how circumlocution generates implicature through indirectness.

(17) "Isn't he very rich?" said Rebecca. "They say all Indian nabobs are enormously rich."

"I believe he has a very large income."

"And is your sister-in-law a nice woman?"

"La! Joseph is not married." said Ameba, laughing again.

When Rebecca and Ameba were talking, Rebecca inquired much about Ameba's brother, Joseph, and what Rebecca cared most was the property and marriage situation about him. Nevertheless, we can see the way that she asked for is quite strategic with implication. Apparently, she asked the former directly but as for the latter, she used an indirect way—she did not directly ask whether he had got married or not but asked whether her sister-in-law was nice or not. Obviously, the indirect query was an implicature of the marriage situation of Joseph. The meaning of the above series of queries, as translated in the heart of this ingenious young woman, was simply this: "If Mr. Joseph Sedley is rich and unmarried, I want to marry him." In fact, all these situations were informed before by Ameba. Then why she asked again? Here, I think, the intention of Rebecca's inquires was not only to confirm but also to imply Ameba that she was interested in Joseph and hoped this message could be transferred to him.

(18) "It seems to me you didn't dislike that wonderful Mr. Joseph last

year," Osborne said kindly.

"How severe of you! Well, entre nous, I didn't break my heart about him; yet if he had asked me to do what you mean by your looks (and very expressive and kind they are too), I wouldn't have said no."

At the mention of Joseph, both Osborne and Rebecca immediately remembered the nearly successful marriage of Rebecca. It was destroyed by Osborne, and of course, Rebecca knew it was he who did it. So the atmosphere then was very unfriendly. In order to prevent offense, Osborne pretended not knowing the reason and used an indirect way to express his opinion. What he really wanted to say was "you like him but why you were separated?" Facing the unfriendly words, Rebecca also responded in an indirect and ironic way. Although she denied her sad feeling in this matter she still turned back in an indirect way. From these words, we know that she was hurt even though it did not break her heart. And the third sentence is more indirect than the previous one.

"What you mean by your looks" actually referred to the proposal. However, she didn't say it out and adopted a prolixity way to indicate it. "I wouldn't say no" obviously means she would say yes but she did not express like that. Using the indirect speech acts in this situation, the speakers can both save their face and imply what they mean.

(19) "I only just warn you." he said to Rawdon Crawley, with a knowing look—he had bought the horse, and lost some score of guineas after diner, "I just warn you—I know women, and counsel you to be on the lookout."

After the talking with Rebecca, George was utterly beaten down. The reason is not that Rebecca was in the right position; but she had managed to put him in the wrong situation, which consequently made him shamefully flee and embarrassed. Though Rebecca had had the better of him, George was above the manners of talebearing or revenging upon a lady at that moment, but he deliberately and cleverly confided to Rawdon Crawly the next day, what is his regarding to Miss Rebecca. In order to pretend his deliberation he repeated twice "I just warn you"; but his behavior told us, of course, he did not want to just give a warning but to deface Rebecca's impression on purpose. And the content of his "warning"—"I know women, and counsel you to be on the outlook" also conveyed much more than what he said. It was the indication that what he once confided to him was right that Miss Rebecca was a sharp one and a dangerous one and a desperate flirt and one should keep away from her.

However, Rawdon did not mind and all the opinions flitted by like a breeze as the novel told us later.

(20) "What do you mean, pretty clear, sir?"

"Why, hang it, sir don't push me too hard. I'm a modest man. I-ah-I don't set up to be a lady-killer; but I do own that she's as devilish fond of me as she can see that with half an eye."

"And you yourself?"

"Why, sir, didn't you order me to marry her, and ain't I a good boy? Haven't our Papas settled it so long?"

These dialogues occurred between George and his father, old Mr. Osborne, who wanted to know his son's attitude toward Ameba. At that time, the business of Ameba's father was in depression and he was managing to run his company. Fully knowing the predicament of his family, this old man definitely wanted his son to break up with the girl and tried to persuade him. However, the young man did not catch his father's meaning and understand the real purpose of his father. Let's look at his way in answering his father indirectly. At first he just replied "pretty clear, sir." But what was "pretty clear", we all, including the old gentleman, could not know. Facing the old father's recapping, the young refused to talk more and mentioned his moral quality and Ameba's deep love but still did not give a direct answer of his own attitude. The meaning he wanted to convey was "since I am a good natured man and she loves me so much, I'll obey your order and be with her." However, the father knew that the most important factor of a love affair was related to both sides and if his son was falling into love with the girl deeply then it was difficult for him to prevent the lovers from getting married, so the old gentleman asked his son: "and you yourself?" To this key inquiry, the cunning young man used three interrogative questions to answer in an indirect way, which implied "everything is settled and you have arranged it for us for so long then there is no need for me to answer such question."

(21) "Do you suppose I have no feeling of self-respect, because I am poor and friendless, and because rich people have none? Do you think, because I am a governess, I have not as much sense, and feeling, and good breeding as you gentle folks in Hampshire? I'm a Montmorency. Do you suppose a Montmorency is not good as a Crawley?"

Hearing the announcement from Mrs. Bute that Rebecca would become his mother-in-law, Rawdon felt unhappy because he loved her too and decided to make clear what the attitude of Rebecca herself was. When he saw her alone, he rallied her about his father's attachment in his graceful way to detect whether his suspicion was true. Of course, the clever young woman got the hints of these words. In order to show her self-respect and her devotion to love, she used anaphor to emphasize her strong indignation towards the matter. She did not say directly that she was a good girl with self-respect and good breeding as the gentle folks, and her origin was also as good as his. In venting all this high qualities of herself, she indicated that she definitely would not accept that old rich man and she would rather endure poverty than shame; neglect than insult from other people. Also it was an implicature to Rawdon that she was an innocent girl who would go after true feelings at the expense of anything else. We all know that is an obvious lie; her real purpose was to win Rawdon ' s love, for she believed that he would inherit a large mount of fortune from his aunt and would be the real rich man in the future.

In order to make my readers more clear about the function of redundancy in the aspect of implicature of Speech Act Theory, I want to provide more examples in direct speech for them in the following. Please have a look of the following one. In the middle of lunch hour, one woman asks another how she likes the hamburger she is eating, and the answer she gets is:

(22) A *hamburger* is a *hamburger*.

From a purely logic perspective, the reply in (22) seems to have no communicative value since it expresses something completely obvious. But it can have possible implicatures. This example and some other apparently pointless expressions like "*mud is mud*" "*business is business*" or "*war is war*" are taken as one kind of redundancy. If they are used in a conversation, clearly the speaker intends to communicate more than what is said. Here, given the opportunity to evaluate the hamburger, we can see that the speaker has responded without an evaluation, thus one implicature is that she has no opinion, either good or bad to express. Depending on other aspects of the context, additional implicatures (for example, the speaker thinks all hamburgers are the same) might be inferred.

Let us study some more examples:

(23) I'm Robert Sampson from Leeds, 28, unmarried.

Supposing a young man introduces himself to a girl at a party like this, the girl would immediately suspect that he has some motive behind, for the introduction is more informative than necessary for the occasion.

(24) A: How did John do his history examination?

B: Oh, not at all well. They asked him things that happened before the poor boy is born.

Here B's answer is obviously over-informative, or redundant, but the redundant answer gives the implicature that the indulgent mother thinks John's failure in the examination is not his fault.

(25) A: What did your sister buy at Sears yesterday?

B_1: She bought a red dress, a green one and a blue one.

B_2: She bought a red dress, she bought a green dress, and she bought a blue dress.

Compared with B_1, B_2 repeats *bought* for three times, and of course the last two are redundant. B_2's speech actually implies that she bought too much.

(26) a. Miss X sang "Home sweet home".

b. Miss X produced a series of sounds that corresponded closely with the score of "Home sweet home".

It is safe to say that Sentence (26) *a* and Sentence (26) *b* share the same deep structure under syntactical analysis. Their difference lies in that in Sentence (26) *b*, the redundant language carries an extra meaning that Miss X's singing is terrible, which is certainly the so-called implicature.

4.3 Functions of Redundancy in Terms of Politeness

Great importance is attached to speaking politely in pragmatics, and redundancy plays a significant role in this aspect, too. When people are trying to speak politely, they will frequently turn to redundant but polite words and expressions.

4.3.1 A Brief Review of Two Theories of Politeness

Leech (1983) deals with politeness by the use of maxims, while Brown & Levinson (1987) analyze politeness as showing awareness of the need to preserve face (public self-image).

Leech's Principle of Politeness is primarily expressed in the negative imperative: Do not offend others, but also includes the positive imperative: Be nice to others. Politeness in communication requires us to adopt strategies of maximizing politc beliefs and minimizing impolite beliefs. Polite beliefs are the term conveniently used for beliefs (expressed or implied) favorable to the other person or unfavorable to the speaker; and impolite beliefs are those which are unfavorable to the other person, or favorable to the speaker. There is therefore a basic asymmetry in polite conversation: whatever is a polite belief for the speaker is impolite for the hearer. This can be illustrated with reference to the following Maxims of Politeness, which tend to go in pairs:

Maxim 1: Tact Maxirn (in impositives and commisives)

(a) Minimize cost to other (b) Maximize benefit to other

Maxim 2: Generosity Maxim (in impositives and commisives)

(a) Minimize benefit to self (b) Maximize cost to self

Maxim 3: Approbation Maxim (in expressives and assertives)

(a) Minimize dispraise of other (b) Maximize praise of other

Maxim 4: Modesty Maxim (in expressives and assertives)

(a) Minimize praise of self (b) Maximize dispraise of self

Maxim 5: Agreement Maxim (inassertives)

(a) Minimize disagreement between self and other

(b) Maximize agreement between self and other

Maxim 6: Sympathy Maxim (inassertives)

(a) Minimize antipathy between self and other

(b) Maximize sympathy between self and other (Leech, 1983)

In Brown & Levinson's Face Saving Theory, politeness involves an awareness to other people's face. It is said that "*Face*" refers to our public self-image. There are two aspects of this self image.

Positive *face* refers to our need to be accepted and liked by others and our need to feel that our social group shares common goals. Positive politeness orients to preserving the positive face of other people. When we use positive politeness we use speech strategies that emphasize our solidarity with the hearer, such as informal pronunciation, shared dialect or slang expressions, nicknames, more frequent reference to speaker and hearer as we, and requests which are less indirect.

Negative *face* refers to our desire for independence of action and our hope not to be imposed on by others. Negative politeness orients to preserving the negative face of other people. This is much more likely if there is a social distance between the speaker and the hearer. When we use negative politeness, we use speech strategies that emphasize our deference for the hearer. Nicknames, slang and informal pronunciation tend to be avoided and requests tend to be more indirect and impersonal, often involving expressions that soften the blow, like *please*, *possibly*, *might*, *probably*, etc.

4.3.2 Functions of Redundancy in Terms of Maxims

Studies show that observing politeness involves proper use of redundancy, and proper use of redundancy will improve the degree of politeness. Either in spoken or written language, redundancy can shorten the distance between communicators and help to create a better communicative circumstance. Examples show that when people are conscious of the Politeness Principle and trying to observe the maxims, their language are more redundant than when they are not. We may compare the following group of sentences:

(27) a. Help me with the luggage.

b. Will you help me with the luggage?

c. Would you mind helping me with the luggage?

From Sentence *a* to Sentence *c*, the length of sentence is in increase, that is to say, the sentence becomes increasingly redundant. At the same time, the sentence becomes increasingly polite because the speaker pays attention to Tact Maxim when speaking out Sentence *b* and Sentence *c*.

In Example (28) Speaker A just wants to say *I want to meet you on the 24 th*, and what Speaker B wants to say is nothing but *That's not suitable. Let's make it the* 31 *st.* But in this conversation, in order to comply to Agreement Maxim, that is, to minimize disagreement between each other, both of them use redundant language to express what they mean.

(28) A: I was wondering if we could meet again on the 24 th.

B: As a matter of fact, I'm afraid that might be a bit difficult as I have to contact one or two colleagues who I do know are out of the country at the moment. Perhaps we could give ourselves an extra week. It is quite important that I have a word with them. Wouldn't the following Thursday, the 31 st , be better?

In each of the following two pairs of sentences between Speaker A and Speaker B, the Speaker B adds an excuse to soften their direct reply, which makes the reply more redundant, however, at the same time, more polite.

(29) A: Are you coming to my party?

B: No, I've got an exam tomorrow.

(30) A: How do you like my painting?

B: I don't have an eye for beauty, I'm afraid. Now let's consider this offer at a party:

(31) A:Has given up alcohol, and B knows this?

B: Would you like a drink? —an orange juice or something?

In Example(31), Speaker B is understood as presupposing that A will want a non-alcoholic drink, so B deliberately cancels the preferred saying of *Would you like a drink*? This is understood as referring to the category of non-alcoholic social drinks *orange juice being a good example* and B politely offers A options within that category. Following is another example, a student's request, taken from a tutorial discussion:

(32) Could we, when you give us our essays back and give us sort of meet or something? Because, I mean, there titles, might be things we want to ask.

Here the student's direct request to the tutor is heard as mitigating its directness by leaving the tutor other options.

4.3.3 Functions of Redundancy in Terms of Face Saving

When people are exercising face saving acts, they inevitably become more redundant than when they are not. George Yule (1996) illustrates it with an example of lending a pen. If a person directly addresses another person as a means of expressing his needs, the direct approach, using imperative forms such as those in (33), is known as bald on record.

(33) a. Give me a pen.

b. Lend me your pen.

While employing a positive politeness strategy, the requester may appeal to a common goal, and even friendship, via expressions such as those in (33a) and (33b). Sometimes it may be preceded by some getting-to-know-you talk, of the kind presented in (33c), designed to establish the necessary common ground for this strategy.

(34) a. How about letting me use your pen?

b. Hey, buddy, I'd appreciate it if you'd let me use your pen.

c. Hi. How's it going? Okay if I sit here? We must be interested in the same crazy stuff. You take a lot of notes too, huh? Say, do me a great favor and let me use one of your pens.

In some other cases, a face saving act is performed via a negative politeness strategy. The most typical form used is a question containing a modal verb such as (34a), or expressions of apology for the imposition, of the type shown in (34b). More elaborate negative politeness work can sometimes be heard in extended talk, often with hesitations, similar to that shown in (34c).

(35) a. Could you lend me a pen?

b. I'm sorry to bother you, but can I ask you for a pen or something?

c. I know you're busy, but might I ask you if-em-if you happen to have an extra pen that I could, you know-eh-maybe borrow?

From the above discussion it is easy to find that no matter which kind of politeness strategy is exercised, it will inevitably lead to more redundancy.

4.4 Functions of Redundancy to Achieve Humor

Redundant language is sometimes intentionally used to express simple ideas, for the purpose of producing a humorous or even ironic effect, as illustrated in Example (36) and (37).

(36) A: Why don't you study hard?

B: The more we study, the more we know. The more we know, the more we forget. The more we forget, the less we know. The less we know, the less we forget. The less we forget, the more we know. So why we study?

B is just going to express the meaning: Study is no use, but he intentionally uses circumlocutory language to express simple meaning, rendering his words plausible and humorous.

(37) Landlord: In a word, when are you going to pay your arrears?

Hard-up author: I will satisfy your demands as soon as I receive the money which the publisher will pay me if I receive the money the publisher will pay me if he accepts the novel I'm going to send him as soon as the work is finished, when I'm about to commence when I have found a suitable subject and necessary inspiration.

This hard-up author has not even got a subject for his writing, while he is imagining that he can pay the rent with the money the publisher will pay him. He deliberately uses redundant language to make up his excuse. In fact, it is the redundant language that gives him the best sarcasm.

4.5 Disambiguating Functions of Redundancy

Ambiguity refers to the fact that a word, a sentence or any linguistic form can be understood or interpreted in more than one way. There are various kinds of causes resulting in ambiguity. It may spring from disordered and muddled thinking, from hasty fitting of words to the thought, from ignorance of the right uses of words, or from the wrong word order, etc. However, in natural language, ambiguity chiefly springs from contradiction between the infiniteness of humans thought and the relative finiteness of the linguistic symbols. It is well known that the world we live in and the things we imagine are infinite, and thus the thought reflecting the world must also be infinite. In language practice, people have to express their infinite thought with the relatively finite linguistic symbols. The arbitrary nature of language decides that there is not always a one-to-one correspondence between expressions and meanings.

Many linguists believe that ambiguity is negative because it undoubtedly causes a certain kind of confusion and unavoidably leads to misunderstanding in the process of communication. M. H. Abrams once described that ambiguity is a defect of style and it is not of any literal value. Kaplan pointed out that ambiguity is a kind of pathology of language itself. William Empson said that ambiguity is the enemy we have to watch. Herbert. J. Grierson even said that ambiguity often makes people more annoyed than misunderstood, thus ambiguity should be avoided in language practice. As has been talked about, ambiguity is inevitable; and as a result, it necessarily becomes a barrier of information to communication, especially to the exchange of pure information. Therefore, in our practical communication, ambiguity, in a sense, should be avoided and removed. We can employ different ways to remove ambiguity, among which redundancy is a very useful one. Sometimes redundant words may provide a clue for the addressee to choose the correct interpretation and remove the other possibly improper or irrelevant interpretations of a given linguistic form. Redundancy thus can help to disambiguate a sentence. For example:

(38) A: Ask the driver what time we get to Birmingham.

B: Could you tell me when we get to Birmingham, please?

C: Don't worry, it's a big place—I don't think it's possible to miss it.

In this dialogue, Speaker B's intention is to know the time they get to Birmingham, but the driver misunderstands it as: when they arrive, tell them. It is ambiguity that leads to the failure of communication. If speaker B said "*Could you tell me the time when we get to Birmingham?*", the seemingly redundant word "time" could have removed ambiguity. And the ambiguity of sentence "The chicken is ready to eat" can be removed by additional words in either of the following two ways:

(39) a. The chicken in the yard is ready to eat.

b. The chicken on the dining-table is ready to eat.

And the sentence "*They went to the bank.*" can be disambiguated in two ways, too.

(40) a. They went to the bank to draw some money.

b. They went to the bank to watch the dragon-boat contest.

4.6 Phatic Functions of Redundancy

As we have discussed in the previous chapter, redundancy, more exactly, phatic communion can be used to perform phatic function. Greetings, farewells, and comments on the weather serve this function. A sentence like "*A nice day, isn't it?*" does not inform the hearer about the weather, for it is a fact he himself can see. But it does make the hearer feel good because the sentence shows that the relationship between them remains what it was. Similarly, when a person asks "*How are you today?*", he is not really interested in the hearer's health, but is expressing good will. Much of the language used for phatic purposes is insincere if taken literally, but to chide it for its insincerity is to miss the point. Useless and redundant as phatic language may appear, its social or interpersonal importance is immediately shown if it is omitted. If one does not say hello to a friend, the consequence can be at times very serious(Hu Zhuanglin, 1987).

In this chapter, we study implicature of redundancy in terms of pragmatic theories. According to Leech (1983), pragmalinguistics is concerned with how to use appropriate linguistic means to perform a speech act and achieve an intended pragmatic effect (instead of linguistic meaning) in a given context. Therefore, the core point of this chapter is how intended meaning—implicature arises from redundancy in different context. To explain implicature of redundancy in contexts, we first make a clear understanding of what is implicature and what is the relationship between the two terms. Generally speaking, a linguistic unit in a certain context may have two meanings: one is the literal meaning and the other is the underline meaning. When there is difference between the two meanings, certain implicatures will result. That is to say, implicature is the distinction between what is said and what is implicated. Implicature can be produced in language use process through various ways and redundancy is one of them. Although redundancy is more troublesome than a brief and direct way for both speakers (writers) and hearers (readers), it is widely used not only in spoken language but also in written language to produce implicatures which can help people achieve certain pragmatic purposes and rhetoric effects. In view of the relationship between redundancy and implicature, this book explores various manifestations of redundancy in terms of representative pragmatic theories which concern Cooperative Principle, Relevance Theory and Indirect Speech Act. Theoretically, the Cooperative Principle can help explain redundancy both in following the maxims and flouting the maxims. Because implicature is the main concern of this book, we only discuss the flouting of maxims. In the four maxims in Cooperative Principle, there are three maxims related to redundancy: the Quantity Maxim, Relation Maxim and the Manner Maxim. Flouting each maxim will bring different implicatures in certain context. According to Relevance Theory, communication is an ostensive-inferential process, by which hearers get implicatures from speakers. During this process, hearers first make a set of assumptions through the stimulus used by speakers, then find out the optimal relevance between the immediate context and the information, and finally get the intended meaning of the speakers. Discourse markers are one of the stimuli that can reduce the effort when people look for the optimal relevance between the context and the information. They play a role of instruction, which can exclude some impossible or irrelevant assumptions and direct the hearers to choose the optimal assumption and then get the only right understanding of the utterance. Based on the previous studies, we conclude the shared characteristics of indirect speech acts: there is difference between literal meaning and underline meaning. And in fact those differences are the implicatures produced by speakers or writers. Circumlocution, one of the manifestations of redundancy, is a typical indirect speech act because it can bring implicatures through a roundabout way.

本章从语用角度阐述了冗余的积极功能,因为本质上冗余与语言的日常使用密切相关。从语用角度来看,冗余与合作原则、礼貌和言语行为理论等有着不可分割的联系。恰当地使用冗余一方面有助于遵守合作原则,另一方面也可以为了特殊的含义而无视合作原则。此外,冗余有助于体现语言中的礼貌,甚至可以在语言表达中创造美感。值得一提的是,冗余也经常用于间接言语行为中。此外,冗余还能产生幽默效果,消除句子的歧义,实现交际功能。从修辞的角度来看,重复是一种冗余,也是一种修辞格,在文学作品中被广泛使用以达到不同的效果。

Chapter 5 Redundancy in Text

Based on the interpretation in terms of pragmatic theories, redundancy can help people to produce and comprehend implicatures as discussed in the former chapter. However, that is not the only function of redundancy, because it also makes great contribution to text, which includes rhetoric functions and textual functions. Text refers to any natural language which is free from syntactic rules to express complete meaning in certain context. The aim of it is to finish specific communication task or perform a certain act (Hu Zhuanglin, 2003). According to Leech & Short (2001), text is linguistic communication seen simply as a message coded in its auditory or visual medium, which includes both spoken communication and written communication. Redundancy in a text can not only produce the active rhetoric effect of emphasis, elicit emotions and build images, but also strengthen the textual function of unity and coherence. Now, Let us see how these functions are achieved in the text of *Vanity Fair*.

5.1 Rhetoric Effects

Rhetoric effects achieved by redundancy are mainly through all kinds of repetition. Generally speaking, repetition can be divided into immediate repetition and intermittent repetition, both of which have certain kind of rhetoric functions. Feng Cuihua (2005) thinks that in immediate repetition, each time a word is repeated it acquires added significance and even new implications, emphasizing a mood or feeling, or a feature of something. And the function of intermittent repetition is to emphasize a quality or feature of something, and to give a cohesive effect to mood or thought in long passage. According to Hu Shuzhong (1993), both modern English and Chinese often use repetition to express a strong feeling, a sense of urgency and highlight a certain meaning of something. That is the truth, because people usually use repetition for diverse purposes, the chief of which are emphasizing the main point, expressing emotions and attitudes, and describing vivid images.

5.1.1 Emphatic Effect

Emphasis and enforcement are two of the major functions of repetition, which can emphasize certain feelings and moods or the main point that a speaker or a writer want to express. For instance:

(1) Good night, a *thousand*, *thousand*, *thousand* kisses!

That is an end of Rebecca's letter to Ameba. The reason why three immediate "thousand" used here by her was that Rebecca wanted to show her deep love to the receiver. It seemed that one simple "thousand" was not enough to express her feelings and more than one had to be used for emphasis of her kindness. In fact, one "thousand" is big enough and we all know she was saying that with her tongue in her cheek. The repetition here is a speaking strategy for her insincere feeling.

(2) "How kind you all axe to me! *All.*" she added, with a laugh, "except you, Mr. Joseph."

When Joseph made his second appearance after several days' panic,

Rebecca was certainly very happy. In order to encourage Joseph she decided to say something to let him feel easy. So she deliberately mentioned the trick Joseph made to her, which he himself thought was very great. At the mention of that, she repeated the word "all" to emphasize everyone in his family who was kind to her but he was exclusive. Of course, here, Rebecca just wanted to make a small joke on Joseph and to improve their relationship.

(3) *All* the savants were there in the hall—*all* the dear friend—*all* the young ladies—the dancing-master who had just arrived; and there was such a scuffing, *and* hugging, *and* kissing, *and* crying, with the hysterical YOOPS of Miss Swartz, the parlour boarder, from her room, as no pen can depict, and as the tender heart would faro pass over. The embracing was over; they parted—that is, Miss Sedley parted from her friends. Miss Sharp had demurely entered the carriage some minutes before. Nobody cried for leaving HER.

This was the scene when Ameba and Rebecca was leaving the school and parted from their friends. The author there used three "all" to describe the occasion, which could just say "all the people in that school came". If so, we could not see how spectacular the scene was because the four repetitive "all" were used to emphasize none of the people there was absent. And later, the three "and" were also used to emphasize their deep love for Ameba and reluctance to part with her. All the emphasis there made a great contrast with the parting scene of Rebecca, during which she entered the carriage some minutes before the parting with nobody saying "goodbye". If there was no such emphasis, there was no such great contrasting effect. Once again, we have a look of an example used in the former chapter:

(4) There was that in Rawdon's face which caused Becky to fling her-

self before him. "*I am innocent*, Rawdon," she said; "before God, *I am innocent.*" *She clung hold of his coat, of his hands; her own were all covered with serpents, and rings, and baubles.* "*I am innocent.* Say *I am innocent*," she said to Lord Steyne. He thought a trap had been laid for him, and was as furious with the wife as with the husband. "*You innocent*! Damn you," he screamed out. "*You innocent*! Why every trinket you have on your body is paid for by me. I have given you thousands of pounds, which this fellow has spent and for which he has sold you. *Innocent*, by-! You're as *innocent* as your mother, the ballet-girl, and your husband the bully. Don't think to frighten me as you have done others. Make way, sir, and let me pass".

When the misconduct between Rebecca and Lord Steyne was discovered by Rawdon face to face, she was frightened and asked the Lord to prove her innocence. She repeated "I am innocent" for four times, which was both the emphasis of her "innocence" to her husband and the request of her lover's help. Of course, all three people involved and readers know that was a lie. To her lover's thought, it was a trap of the couples to cheat him for his money, which made the Lord furious. He also used four repeated "innocent" to fight back. That was a strong satire, through which we all can get the implicature of his words—to emphasize her innocence was pretended and she was a slut in fact. By the way, those repeated words also were a venting of the Lord's fury, which is the expressive function of repetition as will be discussed below.

5.1.2 Expressive Effect

Repetition can also be used to express all kinds of emotion and attitudes of a speaker or a writer such as hatred, dissatisfied, delight, eager and so on.

(5) "Why, will the black footman tell tales?" cried Miss Rebecca, laughing. "He may go back and tell Miss Pinkerton that I hate her with all my soul; *and I wish* he would; *and I wish* I had a means of proving it, too. For two years *I have* only had insults and outrage from her. *I have* been treated worse than any servant in the kitchen. *I have* never had a friend or a kind word, except from you. *I have* been made to tend the little girls in the lower schoolroom, and to talk French to the Misses, until I grew sick of my mother tongue. But that talking French to Miss Pinkerton was capital fun, wasn't it? She doesn't know a word of French, and was too proud to confess it. I believe it was that which made her part with me; and so thank Heaven for French. Vive la France! *Vive* I'Empereur! *Vive* Bonaparte!"

"O *Rebecca*, *Rebecca*, for shame!" cried Miss Sedley...

The first paragraph is the complaints from Rebecca about Miss Pinkerton. Anaphora and parallelism are used in her utterances to express her strong dissatisfaction. First, she used two "I wish" to express her desire—let her "enemy" know exactly what she was thinking, which revealed that she harbored bitter hatred feeling toward Miss Pinkerton. After that, she gave an account of her bad and unfair treatment got from the headmistress, which were the reasons for her revenging thought. And finally she even used three "vive" phrases to thank the fascist dictatorship. From all those forceful sentences, we can see how agitated and dissatisfied she was to Miss Pinkerton at that place. On the contrary, facing those utterances, Miss Sedley was almost astonished and she cried to her friend to stop eagerly with two "Rebecca", the first one can be seen as the name but the second repetitive one was the requirement for shutting up in urgency. For this was the greatest blasphemy Rebecca had as yet uttered; and in those days, in England, to say that was as much as to say long live a demon.

(6) In order to maintain authority in her school, it became necessary to remove *this* rebel, *this* monster, *this* serpent, *this* firebrand...

The same to Rebecca, Miss Pinkerton—the headmistress also disliked her treasonous and arrogant student in her school. In her eyes, Rebecca was just as bad as an eyesore. To express the disgusted feeling in Miss Pinkerton's heart, the author had used the demonstrative pronoun "this" for four times, the "this" used again and again could be taken off at least three ones or even be replaced by a much briefer phrase like "evil woman". If so, there was no grammar error in the sentence and still would not affect readers' understanding of the feeling of Miss Pinkerton to Rebecca, however, the expressive effect would be weakened so much that it could not express the strong resentful feelings.

(7) "How they cringe and bow to that Creole, because of her hundred thousand pounds! *I am* a thousand times cleverer and more charming than that creature, *for* all her wealth, *I am* as well bred as the Earl's granddaughter, *for* all her fine pedigree, *and yet* every one passes me by here. *And yet*, when I was at my father's, did not the men give up their gayest balls and parties in order to pass the evening with me?"

Those are the thoughts of Rebecca towards her only friend—Ameba, who had a very happy and rich family and highly respected by others. Although Ameba was the only person to whom she could attach herself in the least, the happiness and superior advantages around her gave Rebecca in expressive pangs of envy. In fact, from all the repetitive words we can feel how strong the envious feeling was. With such intense envy, Rebecca determined at any rate to get free from the prison-like school and began to make plans and act for her future. Just because of that, there came the following story of this novel.

Similarly, William Shakespeare also fovored this kind of redundancy to reinforce his dramatic effect. Please have a look at the following example:

(8) When we are born, we cry that we are come, to this stage of fools. This' a good block!

It were a delicate stratagem to shoe.

A troop of horse with felt; I'll put it in proof,

And when I have stol'n upon these sons-in-law,

Then, *Kill*, *kill*, *kill*, *kill*, *kill*, *kill*!

(*King Lear*)

When the old King Lear knew that his favored daughters with their husbands had not only betrayed him, but even wanted to put him into death, he was very angry. In the above lines, the word "kill" has been repeated for six times, which strongly expresses this character's strong will for revenge and disappointment. Actually, this kind of redundancy can be easily found in this great tragedy. For example, when the news comes to King Lear that his beloved youngest daughter was killed in the prison, he could not help controlling himself, painfully speaking out "Thou'll come no more, never, never, never, never" to tell the spectator his remorse and anguish. Similar examples exist here and there in Shakespeare's dramas, and these definitely reinforce the dramatic effect of his works and further consolidate the artistic status in the world of literature.

5.1.3 Descriptive Effect

Besides the emphatic and expressive functions, repetition and implication also can help to vividly describe an image or act, which includes figures, surroundings, psychological activity and so on. Let us have a look at some examples:

(9) "*Is the girl making fun of me*?" he thought, and straightway he bounced towards the bell, and was for retreating, as we have seen, when his father's jokes and his mother's entreaties caused him to pause and stay where he was. He conducted the young lady down to dinner in a dubious and agitated frame of mind. "Dose she really think I am handsome?" thought he, "*or is she only making game of me*?"...

The italic utterances were the repetitive description of Joseph's psychological activity. Rebecca's praise of his handsome looking thrilled through every fiber of his big body and made it tingle with pleasure. However, he still felt dubious and could not believe that was true. The repetitive description of his thought let us see the contradiction in his mind—on one side, it was apparently pleasure; on the other side, it was obviously doubt. If there were no such recurrences, the image of this man certainly would not be so funny and vivid and therefore it could not give readers such a deep impression.

(10) As the only endowments with which nature had gifted Lady Crawley were those of pink cheeks and a white skin, and as she had no sort of character, *nor* talents, *nor* opinions, *nor* occupations, *nor* amusements, *nor* that vigor of soul and ferocity of temper which often falls to the lot of entirely foolish women. Her hold upon Sir Pitt's affections was not very great.

In order to depict an unattractive character—Lady Crawley, the author used five "nor" to show her commonplaceness and inability. Neither from the appearance nor from the inner was Mrs. Crawley a charming woman at least to her husband. All the "nor" produced a vivid image of a dull and boring character. That was just a flagrant contrast with Rebecca, to whom the ordinary woman's husband liked so much that he immediately made a proposal after her death. If the author omitted these "nor" and adopted a brief way to describe without a repetitive device, the figure's characteristics could not be so prominent and the contrasting effect would not be so distinct.

(11) It was Ameba, but how changed from the fresh and comely girl Osborne knew. *Her* face was white and thin. *Her* pretty brown hair was parted under a widow's cap—the poor child. *Her* eyes were fixed, and looking nowhere.

After George's death in the war, Ameba nearly lost herself. She changed so much that even the old Osborne could not recognize her. From the description of her appearance, we can see how great the hurt she got from her husband's death. "her face" "her hair" and "her eyes" all lost the color they used to have: her face blushed with rosy health, her lips with the freshest of smiles, and she had a pair of eyes which sparkled with the brightest and honest good humor, just as described in the early chapter. Compared with the obviously disparate descriptions, we know Ameba had suffered a lot.

5.2 Textual Functions

The textual function refers to the fact that language has mechanisms to make any stretch of spoken or written discourse into a coherent and unified text and make a living message different from a random list of sentences. (*Linguistics: A Course Book* by Hu zhuanglin, Liu Runqing and Li Yanfu) In a good designed text, unity and coherence are required not only for the whole essay but also for a sentence or a paragraph. Since the analyzed text is a long novel, this book will take paragraphs as examples to illustrate the functions achieved by redundancy, mainly concerning the repetition and discourse markers.

5.2.1 Unity

According to Hu Shuzhong (2004), text unity means that all parts of a text should relate to the core meaning and connect with each other. In other words, if a paragraph develops more than one idea, it fails to have unity. Paragraph unity means that all the sentences in the paragraph illustrate or explain the main idea, and not any other idea. Every element in a paragraph must be directly and clearly tied into the central theme, just as each paragraph must be linked to the overall intention of the essay. As for redundancy, repetition and implication can help to achieve unity. For instance:

(12) "*Books*!" cried the elder lady indignantly, "*Books*, when the whole house wants bread! Books, when to keep you and your son in luxury, and your dear father out of goal, I've sold every trinket I had, the India shawl from my back even down to the very spoons, that our tradesmen mightn't insult us, and that Mr. Clapp, which indeed he is justly entitled, being not a hard landlord, and break my heart with your books and that boy of yours, whom you are mining, though part with him you will not. Oh, Ameba, may God send you a more dutiful child than I have had! There's Jos, deserts his father in his old age and there's George, who might be provided for, and who might be rich, going to school like a lord, with a gold watch and chain round his neck—while my dear, dear old man is without a sh—shilling."

After Osborne's death, Ameba cared for nothing or nobody except George, her son. In order to make little George happy, she sold her ornaments for money and bought some books for him, which were he longed for. But at that time the whole family fell deeper and deeper into trouble, so when her mother, Mrs. Sedley, saw those books, she was very angry and scolded Ameba in a hysteric way for buying them when the whole family was short for bread. Even though, in the indignant blame, there was some information about Joseph and the imagination of little George's future, which seemed irrelevant to this matter, we know from the repetition of the word "books" that, all she wanted to scold was that Ameba should not have kept the books. She should care about others and should buy some food for the whole family. In other words, the repetitive "books" made all the utterances unified and gave prominent to the core meaning of what the old lady wanted to say.

(13) Here, before long, Becky received not only "*the best*" foreigners, but some of the best English people too. I don't mean the most virtuous, or indeed the least virtuous, or the cleverest, or the richest, or the best born, but "*the best*," —in a word, people about whom there is no question—such as the great Lady Fitz-Wills, that Patron Saint of Almack's, the great Lady Slowborn, the great Lady Grizzel Macbeth (she was Lady G. Glowry, daughter of Lord Grey of Glowry), and the like. When the Countess of Fitz-Willis (her Ladyship is of the Kingstreet family, see Debrett and Burke) takes up a person, he or she is safe. *There is no question about them any more.* Not that my Lady Fitz-Willis is any better than anybody else, being, on the contrary, a faded person, fifty-seven years of age, and neither handsome, nor wealthy, nor entertaining; *but it is agreed on all sides that she is of the "best people."* Those who go to her are of the best: *The most important fact was known all over London that night... In a word, she was admitted to be among the "best" people.*

The above paragraph was a description of Becky's position, which changed from a petty and low class to an honorable one in the rank of a fashion society. After her appearance at Lord Steyne's private and select parties, the claims of that estimable woman as regards to fashion were settled. In the whole paragraph, the author mentioned many noble persons who once looked down upon or neglected Becky, and described their changed attitude towards Becky from an old grudge to Lady Steyne. Because of all those things, this paragraph seems too long and wordy. In order to emphasize the core meaning and give readers a clear and unified impression, the author used the device of repetition of the key words and the vital information. Turn to the paragraph again, we find that the key word "best" was repeated for seven times in different places, which emphasized that Rebecca belonged to the best class then; and the core idea of this paragraph—she was admitted to be among the "best" people was entailed in five different sentences. All the repetition of key word and the recurrence of the core idea made the whole paragraph unified and clear. Therefore, all those inserted things worked as great examples to support the subject of the topic rather than affected the core meaning of the whole paragraph.

5.2.2 Cohesion

As we have seen, an important quality of an effective paragraph is unity. A unified paragraph sticks to one topic from start to end, with every sentence contributing to the central purpose and main idea of that paragraph. But unity alone is not enough to make a paragraph clear. It must also have coherence. Coherence refers to connection and organization. It is the unbroken forward movement (Li Shiping, 2002). In other words, a coherent paragraph is one in which the ideas are put in the right order with the right connecting words so that it is easy for the reader to follow your thought. Therefore, a strong paragraph is more than just a collection of loose sentences. Those sentences need to be clearly connected so that readers can follow along and recognize how one detail leads to the next. A paragraph with clearly connected sentences is said to be coherent which can be achieved through logical order of your ideas, transitional words and phrases (another saying for discourse markers), repeated key terms and parallelism (Zhou Guoqing, 2004). As redundancy is concerned, we take some example from *Vanity Fair* to see how repetition and discourse markers make contribution to coherence.

(14) "I suppose I must." said Miss Sharp calmly, *and* much to the wonder of Miss Jemima; *and* the latter having knocked at the door, *and* receiving permission to come in, Miss Sharp advanced in a very unconnected manner, *and* said in French, *and* with a perfect accent, "Mademoiselle, jeviens vous faire mes adieux."

When Rebecca was going to leave the school, Miss Jemima asked her to say goodbye to Miss Pinkerton. Rebecca did prepare to do that, which was unexpected to the latter. However, the process seemed unusual and disconnected. In order to make the paragraph coherent, the author used five "and" to connect a series of seemingly irrelevant sentences, which in fact indicated the order of the activities. The first "and" connected the words of Rebecca and the attitude of Miss Jemima. The second "and" connected the reorganization of the former's reply and the latter's instruction to the headmistress. Then the third "and" indicated they got the permission of entering. But when Rebecca entered the room, her manner was unconnected; therefore, to emphasize that unnatural and arrogant manners, the author still used two "and" to connect. With this analysis, we know that it is the repetitive "and" that makes the whole paragraph coherent. If they are omitted, the whole paragraph will become a series of loose sentences.

(15) "What is birth, my dear!" she would say to Rebecca—"*Look at* my brother Pitt; *look at* the Huddlestons, who have been here since Henry II; *look at* poor Bute at the parsonage—is any one of them *equal* to you in intelligence or breeding? *Equal* to you—they are not even *equal* to poor dear Briggs, my companion, or Bowls, my butler. You, *my love*, are a little paragon—positively a little jewel—you have more brains than half the shire—if merit had its reward you ought to be a *Duchess*—no, there *ought to* be no *duchesses* at all—but you *ought to* have no superior, and I consider you, *my love*, as my *equal* in every aspect; *and*—will you put some coals on the fire, my dear; *and* will you pick this dress of mine, *and* alter it, you who can do it so well?" So this old philanthropist used to make her equal run of her errands, execute her millinery, *and* read her to sleep with French novels, every night.

Miss Crawley was an ultra-liberal in opinions and always expresses her opinions in the most candid manner. The above paragraph was her utterances to Rebecca, which include the evaluation of herself to the latter and the things she wanted Rebecca to do for her. Such a long paragraph must make the hearers and readers at a loss if it is not well organized. However, the talkative old lady designed her discourse very well. First, she used anaphora to connect the three unrelated people together to make a comparison with Rebecca, which she thought none of the noble men could be equal to the latter. Then she repeated "equal" for four times and "duchess" for two times to reach a conclusion that Rebecca was equal to herself because there were no duchesses at all and therefore she was no superior to the latter. All the repetitions were the devices for the old lady to make her assessment coherent. When her opinions about Rebecca was over, she turned her subject to other things—asked the latter to do three things for her, which she used three "and" to connect.

With all the repetitions, the whole speech of the talkative old lady was connected and organized well.

(16) Isidor, the valet, had looked on the very servant was disposing of his master's sulkily, while Osborne's baggage previous to the Captain's departure: *for in the first place* he hated Mr. Osborne, whose conduct to him, and to all inferior, was generally overbearing (nor does the continental domestic like to be treated with insolence as our better-tempered servants do), *and secondly*, he was angry that so many valuables should be removed from under his hands, to fall into other people's possession when the English discomfiture should arrive. Of this defeated he and a vast number of other persons in Brussels and Belgium did not make the slightest doubt. The almost universal belief was, that the Emperor would divide the Prussian and English armies, annihilate one after the other, and march into Brussels before three days were over when all the movables of his present masters, who would be killed, or fugitives, or prisoners, would lawfully become the property of Monsieur Isidor.

As mentioned before, coherence also can be achieved by discourse markers, which signal the curve and direction of thoughts as you read through the paragraph. With them, readers can be prepared for new information and relate them to the old ones. That is to say, the discourse markers can help readers go across from one idea to another and make a coherent comprehension of the whole paragraph. The above example shows how the paragraph is made smoothly with the help of discourse markers—"in the first place" and "secondly", which are the indication of order. Why the servant looked so sulky? The phrase "in the first place" indicated the most important reason—he hated his master; and "secondly" indicated the relative less important reason—he was angry that so many valuables would fall into other people's possession but not his own when they were defeated. And that thought led to the belief of most people then, with which he imagined his master he hated to be in disastrous end and all the property would lawfully become his own, making him a Monsieur. With the help of these guiding words and phrases we get a full understanding of this paragraph. After reading, we can see how people treated each other and what the relationship in this novel—*Vanity Fair* was.

本章主要讨论语篇中的冗余。从莎士比亚的戏剧《名利场》以及日常会话中援引大量实例来说明冗余在使用时可以实现不同的效果,如强调效果、表达效果和描述效果,以及语篇功能的统一和衔接。这些例子说明,在语言使用方面,说话者和作者从他们的角度出发,会有意识或无意识地考虑他们想要表达的内容,用冗余来达到某种语用目的。

Chapter 6 Implicit Reasons for the Existence of Redundancy

Redundancy is a relatively more troublesome way for communication because it requires more effort to both sides in that process. However, why is this language phenomenon still common and even popular on some occasions? This book has explained it in terms of pragmatic theories from the aspect of implicature and discussed the distinguished value of it in text. From those analyses, we know redundancy contributes a lot to pragmatic and rhetoric fields. However, that is not the only reason for its prevalence. We find that there are some implicit reasons for its existence and this book will make an exploration on them from several aspects: motivation, context, function, psychology, style, culture and society.

6.1 Motivational Factors

According to the achievements in neurolinguistics, (Wang Dechun, 1997) the production of language comes from the expression motivation of speakers. There are various kinds of motivations such as expressing thought, wish, feeling, describing, emphasizing and so on. From form Chapters, we see redundancy could help authors to realize ther motivations in writing, which can be counted as rhetoric functions. Besides those motivations in writing, redundancy can also help people achieve different purposes in speaking. For instance, Gillette & Wit (1998) points out that there are five functions for redundancy: enhancing the interpretation of utterance, eliminating ambiguity, making a certain feature prominent, contrasting, emphasizing and creating a poetic function. As for the functions of redundancy in pragmatic field, different people has different opinions, which can be concluded in two categories: one is to ensure the successful transmission of communicative information, in which redundancy can help to produce implicature and avoid ambiguity; the other is to create a certain kind of communication atmosphere such as humor. For instance:

(1) A: Could you please tell me when we arrive in Los Angeles?

B: Don't worry. It's a big place, but I don't think it's possible to miss it I will call you for when we arrive.

A: Oh, I'd like to know the time when we arrive.

B: Sorry, the normal time is 6:15 pm.

This is a dialogue between a passenger and a taxi driver. The failure in communication for the first turn was because the driver misunderstood the word "when". So the passenger had to add "the time" before "when", which clarified the real meaning of the request. The word "when" also referred to time, therefore, the recurrence of these two words was a kind of redundancy, but it was important to ensure the accuracy of information in that situation.

(2) Landlord: In a word, when you are going to pay your arrears?

Hard-up writer: I will satisfy your money as soon as I receive the money which the publisher will pay me if he accepts the novel I'm going to send him as soon as the work is finished, when I'm about to commence when I have found a suitable subject and necessary inspiration.

This roundabout answer of the writer simply meant he could not afford his arrears at that time and even he himself also did not know when he could pay for it. This indirect way he used could ease the atmosphere in some degree on one hand and could create a humorous air which made it easier to be accepted by the landlord on the other hand. As for implicature, it has been discussed in details in the former chapter, so here I would not give more examples to illustrate.

In a word, people can use redundancy to achieve different purposes, which is an important factor for the existing of it although it is not an economic way.

6.2 Contextual Factors

The notion of context is particularly important in pragmatics because it contributes a lot to the meaning of an utterance. Indeed, language use is always situated against a complex background with which it is related in a variety of ways. Among the factors that affect the degree of redundancy, context is also the most important and active one. In a broad sense, there exist two types of contexts: linguistic context and non-linguistic context. Linguistic context is closely relevant to the linguistic symbols. It usually refers to the surrounding words. Non-linguistic context is certainly more complicated, including situational contexts, social contexts, and cultural contexts, etc. To be more specific, non-linguistic context is generally considered as constituted by the common knowledge shared by the speaker and the hearer. It includes background knowledge, i. e. knowledge of the world, knowledge specific to the situation of communication, as well as knowledge of the language they use. No matter what kind of context is concerned, it has great influence on the degree of redundancy. Specific context may provide a clue for the speaker or writer to choose the most appropriate way of expression, for example, to add some information or to omit some information. In other words, context performs screening function on language. That is to say, when we speak or write, we do not have to repeat information which has already existed in context. If we do, redundancy will occur.

First let us look at an example of linguistic context.

(3) *She* elbowed her way to get off the bus. *She* dashed to the lake. *She* stood on the bank, breathing heavily, tears filling her eyes. *She* could see no sign of her lovely little boy. *She* took off her coat and shoes. *She* jumped into the water, spreading her hands under the water, and moving round and round, tying to feel for the child but to no avail. *She* moved forward and felt all round. Suddenly *she* touched his foot but it escaped her fingers. *She* made a desperate effort to grasp it.

In the above paragraph the word "*she*" appears for nine times. Except the "*she*" at the beginning, the other eight are regarded as redundant because the first "*she*" is part of linguistic contexts and it decides that the following ones add nothing new and therefore should be omitted. Let us illustrate this with another example, this time, of non-linguistic contexts.

(4) (in a book store)

Customer: A *Readers' Digest*, please.

The customer wants to buy a *Readers' Digest* in the bookstore. He just says *A Readers' Digest*, *please*, then the bookseller gets to know that he wants to buy this magazine. Here both the customer and the bookseller share such information: a) People come to a bookstore to buy books or magazines or newspapers; b) There is *Readers' Digest* for sale in this bookstore; and c) *Readers' Digest* is the magazine that both of them know. With the help of this context, which is, in this case, a kind of shared knowledge, the customer just says "*A Readers' Digest, please*" instead of "*I want to buy a copy of Readers' Digest*", resulting in the great reduction of redundancy. This example can suggest, on the other hand, that less shared knowledge between the speaker or writer and the listener or reader will require more redundancy.

6.3 Functional Factors

Language has to serve various functions as there are different types of occasions for using it. Language has developed into several variables according to the different functions to be performed, and every variable has got its own characteristics. Different functions language performs will lead to different degree of redundancy. The following is a comparison of degree of redundancy between legal documents and news reports among different languages.

Fig. 6-1 (From Darian, S. 1979)

	Russia	Polish	German	French	English
Legal documents	0.668	0.676	0.635	0.672	0.675
News reports	0.512	0.591	0.545	0.573	0.518

Now we are going to discuss these two typical variables: legal English and journalistic English. We hope that through the analysis of these two variables, we can shed some light on how functional factors influence the degree of redundancy.

6.3.1 Legal English

Legal English has its unique social function, that is, imposition of obligations and conferring of rights. This determines that legal English is characterized by conservativeness and complexity. Legal English always takes on identifying linguistic forms, and the language of legal English must be accurate, exact and precise. That is to say, anything legal must be expressed and understood without any loss or misunderstanding. So most legal documents are extremely lengthy and redundant. In example (5), a simple sentence "Have an orange" can be written as a circumfluous and much longer sentence in legal English.

(5) a. Have an orange.

b. I hereby give and convey to you, all and singular, my estate interests, right, title, claim and advantages of and in the orange, together with all rind, juice, pulp and pits, and all rights and advantages therein... anything hereinbefore or hereinafter, or in any other deed or deeds, instrument or instruments of whatever nature or kind whatsoever, to the contrary, in any wise, notwithstanding(Hou Weirui, 1988).

Legal English contains only complete and major sentences. Both the incomplete sentences and minor sentences are scarce in legal English. "It is a characteristic legal habit to conflate, by means of an array of subordinating devices, sections of language which would elsewhere be much more likely to appear as separate sentences." (Crystal David & Davy Derek, 1969). As a result, legal sentences are usually complicated compound sentences capable of standing alone. In legal documents, even in those which are divided into several sentences, the sentences still tend to be extremely long.

Moreover, there are abundant lexical repetitions, which are a kind of redundancy, in legal English. Concerning with exactness of reference, draftsmen of legal documents seldom use anaphoric links between sentences except occasional introductory adverbials, for instance, whereof. So almost the only formal linkage to be found between the long and self-sufficient sentences is perhaps the repetition of lexical items. Even within a sentence structure, pronoun reference and anaphora are also scarce in legal English. This is simply due to the fact that their use could raise genuine confusion.

Coordination at all levels and of all kinds is very common in legal English. Some of the most characteristic collocations are those in which synonyms or near-synonyms are coordinated, sometimes in quite extensive lists, but more usually in pairs, for instance, *made and signed*, *terms and conditions*, *agent and collector*, *able and willing*, *covenants and agreements*, *purchase or sell*, *stipulations reservation and covenants*. In some cases, a native English word is complemented by a borrowed French equivalent, such as *goods and chattels*. Structures, for instance, adverbial elements are also often coordinated, such as *on the expiration*... or on *the previous death*, *subject to any authorized endorsement*... *and to the production*... *on credit or without such payment*. This kind of coordination, in some degree, is also a kind of repetition, and of course belongs to redundancy.

To achieve exactness and to evade any possible misinterpretation, legal English is to be extremely detailed in expression lest there should arise anything disputable concerning the stipulations on rights or obligations. This will also lead to redundancy. In the following two examples, two simple words "person" and "occupying" are explained in a very redundant way.

(6) Person—means a natural person and not a corporation, partnership, association or business name

(7) Occupying (the owned motor vehicle)— means in or upon or entering into or alighting from (the owned motor vehicle)

To sum up, the extremely long sentences, preference for lexical repetition, wide use of coordination, together with the meticulous way of expression lead to the redundancy and wordiness of legal English.

6.3.2 Journalistic English

The application of English to news coverage has evolved a variable of its own, which is journalistic English. Journalistic English is characterized by the ABC principle, which is accuracy in content, brevity in diction and clarity in sentence making and logic relation (Feng Qinhua, 2001). It is demanded that as much news as possible be carried in the limited space of a newspaper, so the language of journalistic English is concise and succinct, and therefore the degree of redundancy is relatively low in journalistic English.

To achieve brevity and save space, the news reporter often leaves out whatever can be omitted in writing. As a result, such condensed words as initialisms, acronyms and clipped words can be found almost everywhere in English newspapers. For instance, *mod* (*modern*), *pop* (*popular*), *Govt.* (*Government*), *Capt.* (*Capital*), *Lab* (*labor*), *Lib* (*liberal*), *ad.* (*advertisement*), *Yiets* (*Vietnamese*), *NATO* (*North Atlantic Treaty Organization*), *ETV* (*Educational Television*), *CID* (*Criminal Investigation Department*), *GCE* (*General Certificate of Education*). Condensed words are, of course, less redundant than whole words because they occupy less space and can still be understood by those people who often read newspapers.

In modern English there is a tendency to put before nouns more and more modifications that are normally put after nouns. This linguistic phenomenon is especially conspicuous in journalistic English. Because pre-modification of nominal heads is far more compact than post-modification, it can reduce the degree of redundancy, as in Examples (8) and(9).

(8)a. Britain's round-the-world yachtsmen

b. the yachtsmen from Britain who plan to go round the world

(9)a. 200-meter-long flood prevention dyke

b. dyke of 200 meters long built for the prevention of flood

Another way of saving space is deletion, that is, to eliminate superfluous words. This is especially common in headlines. Definite or indefinite articles, pronouns, link verbs and auxiliary verbs are often among the elements to be dropped. Undoubtedly, this kind of deletion will reduce the degree of redundancy. Let us study the following examples.

(10) Blaze at Charity Bonfire Damages Warehouses (= A Blaze at a Charity Bonfire Damages Warehouses)

(11) Judge Reverses the Driving Decision

(= The Judge Reverses the Driving Decision)

(12) Irish Group Kills Ex-chief.

(= Irish Group Kills its Ex-chief.)

(13) Anne and Baby are Well.

(= Anne and Her Baby are Well.)

(14) Labor Women at Crossroads

(= Labor Women Are at Crossroads)

(15) 383 Americans Dead in Guyana Sect Commune

(= 383 Americans Are Dead in Guyana Sect Commune)

Still for the purpose of saving space, news reporters even use punctuation instead of conjunction, parenthesis instead of clause. This definitely makes language less redundant. For instance, using comma, will make language less redundant. For instance,

(16) a. Belgium supports francs, denies it will quit "snake".

b. Belgium supports francs and denies it will quit "snake".

(17) a. There were immediate suspicious that Bill Clinton's decision last week to airdrop relief supplies over Bosnia (a step that had seemed like a low-risk humanitarian gesture) might have been answered in thunder by the Serbs.

b. There were immediate suspicious that Bill Clinton's decision last week to airdrop relief supplies over Bosnia, which was a step that had seemed like a low-risk humanitarian gesture, might have been answered in thunder by the Serbs.

The principle of journalistic English is brevity and clarity. The expression should be simple but accurate. We can compare the two sentences in Examples (18) and(19).

(18) a. The man decided after a great deal of consideration that it was best to act then and there. (redundant)

b. The man finally decided to act immediately. (terse)

(19) a. This problem is recognized as a very difficult one and its solution is baffling to the best mathematicians. (redundant)

b. This very difficult problem baffles the best mathematicians. (terse)

Needless to say, sentence *b* is less redundant than sentence *a*, and therefore is more preferred in journalistic English. From the above discussion we can see, because of the employment of clippings, acronyms, pre-modification and deletion, the degree of redundancy in journalistic English is relatively low.

6.4 Psychological Factors

In language communication, the production and interpretation are closely related to social psychology. According to it, "language was not created until the highest stage of humans being's psychology had developed into." (Wu Liquan, 2002). That is to say, language is constricted by humans psychology. Redundancy as one prevailing language phenomenon also has a close relationship to psychology. The applying of redundancy relates to humans psychological needs, which are divided into five groups by American psychologist Maslow, one of which is the need for respect (Maslow, 1962). Since identification and respect are the common psychological needs of humans beings, in communication process we must take them into consideration. Respect involves two sides: both speakers and hearers in communication; therefore the speaker should not only consider the respect for himself but also that for others. In order to follow that, speakers will try their best to express in a polite and euphemistic way. Using redundancy is one of the most important ways for politeness and euphemism. For instance:

(20) A: Are you free tonight?

B: What's up?

A: Would you like to see a film with me?

B: Oh, I'd like to but I have to prepare for my exams next week.

In the above example, both A and B were following the rule of politeness, because they both expressed themselves in a roundabout way rather than a direct way. A was afraid to be refused and in order to keep face for himself, he asked if she was free or not at the beginning. Meanwhile, in case of offending A's self-respect, B gave a reason, maybe excuse, why she could not go.

Let us take criticizing for another example (Sun Rujian, 2006). Research on psychology show that when people face direct criticizing, both body and mind will be in a tense condition which will cause negative mental defense. On the contrary, when people face euphemistic criticizing, they could be calm and relaxed which can let them keep a cool mind to listen to the opinion. So euphemistic criticizing also adapts to the need for respect of people. As it is a roundabout and indirect way to express the intention of criticizing, it can make the hearer feel respected and finally accept it.

Redundancy is not only related to social psychology but also associated with individual psychology. Take repetition for example: in communication, people always think only through repetition can they emphasize what they want to express such as the cognition of things, the circumstance around them and certain feelings in their heart, through which they finally reach consensus without misunderstanding and ignorance (Li Xinhua, 2000). So this psychological need makes redundancy popular not only in written language but also in spoken language.

6.5 Stylistic Factors

Style is a complex area in academic debate and there are so many different meanings and explanations about it that we only discuss it in the broadest sense—the distinctive pattern of language features in writing. Hu Shuzhong (2002) concludes that style research include study of how language is applied in a certain context and how language expresses a proposition. Guo Xiumei (1984) points out that the organization of paragraphs, sentence structure (length, economy, variety, and emphasis), the choice of words and figures of speech, even grammar, punctuation and spelling—all of these are matters of style. In a word, style contains the category of articles and the language features of literature type, writers and works. It can be categorized from different perspectives. In terms of the difference in social activities and social relationships, there are legal style, officialese, scientific and technical style, journalese, advertising, phatic communication and so on. According to the degree of formality, Martin Joos (1961) proposed five types: frozen, formal, consultative, casual and intimate. In the frozen style, readers or hearers are not permitted to cross-question the author. Because it is an extremely serious and solemn style and is formed after repeated deliberation, readers can get the underline meaning only through a "frozen process" and legal English belongs to this type. The formal style in most occasions is used for providing information because it is aimed at so many audiences or readers that no response is possible; and officialese most adopts this style. Consultative style is interactive as both sides are involved and most business is transacted in this register. Casual style is used between friends, acquaintance and insiders, the distinctive feature of which is application of ellipsis and slang. The point of intimate style is simply to remind (hardly inform) the addressee of some feelings inside the speaker's heart; this style is usually used in very close relationship such as couples and lovers(QIN Xiubai, 2002).

Redundancy is not born arbitrarily but is required and necessary in certain style. Some researchers have studied the relationship between style and the degree of redundancy, and point out that different styles require different degree of redundancy. Generally speaking, the more formal the language is, the more redundancy it requires. Legal English is universally recognized as the most formal and redundant style; and together with officialdom they even are criticized for their redundant and complex nature in the Plain English Movement. Although there must be some reasons for this movement and it does bring a trend of simplifying, redundancy cannot be eliminated completely for certain reasons and some forms of documents have been fixed which are difficult to change. Let us take legal English and officialdom for example.

To ensure exactness and evade any possible misinterpretation, legal English is to be extremely detailed in expression lest there should arise anything disputable concerning the stipulations on the rights or obligations. On these grounds, Sir Ernest Gowers, who fought against verbose English, explained some of the idiosyncrasies of legal writing and pointed out that the writer of a legal document had to "imagine every possible combination of circumstances to which his words might apply and every conceivable misinterpretation that might be put on them, and to take precautions accordingly. He must avoid all graces, not be afraid of repetitions, or even of identifying them by aforesaids. He must limit by definition words with a penumbra dangerously large, and amplify with a string of near-synonym words with a penumbra dangerously small. He must eschew all pronouns when their antecedents might possibly be open to dispute and generally avoid every possible grammatical ambiguity." (Gowers, *the complete plain words* 1962, cited from Wang Weixin & Paul livesey, 1998). In those detailed and unusual precise descriptions, much of them are redundancies but are necessary. Some legal expressions seem to contain unnecessary repetitions, e. g. *annual and set aside*, *null and void*, *rest*, *residue and remainder*, or *altered*, *modified or transformed*. However, some redundancy is in fact necessary, e. g. the trustee or trustees is needed to show that both the singular and plural are intended. Contrasting with legal English, general English is much briefer and simpler, because it is used in particular contexts in which the reader can be relied on to cooperate by using common sense. Let us see how general English is expressed in legal English in the following three examples.

(21) *Person*—means a natural person and not a corporation, partnership, association or business name.

(22) *Occupying* (the owned motor vehicle)—means in or upon or entering into or alighting from (the owned motor vehicle)

(23) *Have an orange*—I hereby give and convey you, all and singular, my estate and interests, right, title, claim and advantages of and in the said orange, together with all rind, juice, pulp and pits, and all rights and advantages therein... anything hereinbefore or hereinafter, or in any other deed or in deeds, instrument or instruments of whatever nature or kind whatsoever, to the contrary, in any wise, notwithstanding (Hou Weirui, 1988).

Officialdom is the language used by government departments and other official agencies to communicate in writing with the general pubic. It is considered to be a sort of "watered down" legal English and has always been an intermediary between legal English and general English (Huang Weixin, 1998). Although it is very much closer to the latter now, some forms hare been established by usage and even become the international common practice which cannot be changed arbitrarily. And some seemingly wordy expression are reasonable. For instance, the announcement for a diplomatic envoy to leave his or her post is always written according the following form:

(24) Your Excellency,

I have the honor to inform Your Excellency that I shall be leaving... on... and that during my absence Mr... Counselor, will be in charge of the Embassy in the capacity of Charge d'Affaires ad interim.

I avail myself of this opportunity to renew to you the assurances of my highest consideration.

(Signed)

His Excellency Mr. . .

Ambassador Extraordinary and Plenipotentiary of. . .

(place) (Qin Xiubai, 2002)

If it is in a usual situation, we can just say "I'll leave. . . on. . . and Mr. . . . will be in charge of my place ad interim". But this is too informal in an official document.

Quirk(1968) also pointed out that in official documents what seems like jargon is sometimes justifiable. He takes the use of "man" as an example to illustrate, which is described as "male person over the age of twenty-one years". It seems pompously verbose, but "man" can mean so many things that the longer, more precise phrase may be needed in some contexts. Among other things, "man" can mean "member of a team" (as in "we're short a man"), "person regardless of sex" as in "Man is descended from the apes", and even "a piece in a board game". So it is very important to give specific and detailed information about this term to avoid misunderstanding.

From the above analysis, we can see that redundancy is not equal to wordiness and superfluous expression. It is required and necessary in some occasions and in certain styles. Because it can help to clarify the terms and ensure there is no ignorance of something which may result in misunderstanding; and especially in laws redundancy can prevent some people from taking advantage of the loopholes.

6.6 Cultural Factors

It has long been recognized that language is an essential and important part of a given culture and the impact of culture upon a given language is something intrinsic and indispensable. The impact of culture can expand to all levels of language such as vocabulary, grammatical rules, pragmatic principles, writing style, thinking model and so on. Redundancy is a common language phenomenon, so it must be affected or even determined by culture on some occasions. This book will try to explain their relationship from three aspects: the development of vocabulary, thinking model and reasoning things.

In Chinese, we all know the tendency of disyllable from monosyllable in vocabulary. For instance, in ancient Chinese, we often see "zhuo 桌 (desk)" "yi 椅 (chair)" "shi 石 (stone)" "mu 木 (wood)" and "chuang 窗 (window)" in written language, but now we say "zhuozi 桌子" "yizi 椅子" "shitou 石头" "mutou 木头" "chuanghu 窗户". In modern Chinese, the disyllable words are nearly about 70 percent in the whole vocabulary. There is a trend for using of disyllable words. Every one who knows Chinese should understand that the syllables of "zi" "tou" "hu" contain no meaning in those words, that is to say, adding those syllables would not change the meaning of those words. Then why are people willing to adopt a relatively redundant way rather than a brief way to express? According to the research on culture and language, Hu Wenzhong (2004) points out the reason is that Chinese people are favorite for symmetry and harmony in culture.

In terms of thinking model, many scholars have done research on the difference between American people and Japanese people. Satoshi Ishii (1988) compared American thinking model to "bridge style". Because the purpose for American authors or speakers to organize their thoughts is to transmit their intention directly, in order to understand the thoughts, readers or hearers only need to get through from one end to another which just seems like crossing a bridge. While he compared Japanese thinking model to "stepping-stone style". In that model, authors or speakers express their idea in a roundabout and indirect way rather than a direct way, which is like throwing some stepping stones in water to let readers or hearers learn the meaning through them. The American professor Condon concludes four characteristics of Japanese communication style in his book *with Respect to the Japanese: A Guide for American*. One of them is that Americans prefer to come to the point straight and they treat the roundabout way of speaking as unclear in thought train or lack of sincerity. On the contrary, Japanese regard a direct expression as a lack of consideration for others' emotion and they only use it to inferiors in the same group as an order (Hu Wengzhong, 2004). All those differences are caused by the discrepancy of thinking model. The reflection of different thinking models on language is that people from different cultural background will express in different ways. In American's expression, redundancy may be relatively less than that in Japanese's. That is to say, Japanese thinking model gives rise to redundancy in their language.

Redundancy is also affected by the way of reasoning things out. Chinese linguist Zhao Yuanren thinks that about half of the utterance structure belongs to topic-comment type. Topic is the given information and the comment is the unknown information. Linda Wai Ling Young (1982) (Hu Wenzhong, 2004) thinks that, affected directly by that structure, Chinese people often put the conclusion at the end of the speech even though sometimes the reasons are very long, but that is not in agreement with American's expressing habit. In fact, the difference in reasoning way is resulting from the difference in values of American people and Chinese people. Americans think it is more convincing to put the perspective in the beginning; while Chinese value highly of harmorious in humans relations so they think it is important to create a harmorious relationship with hearers at first and then state the material little by little and finally promote their ideas, which certainly will bring about redundancy in the indirect and roundabout statement.

In a word, culture may give rise to redundancy, which may make some language more redundant than other languages. But we cannot judge one way is better than the other just because of redundancy. Both direct and indirect ways are determined by their cultural conceptions. There is no superior or inferior on culture itself.

6.7 Factors of Race and Gender

Racial factors are best shown in Black English. With the drop of many inflections, morphology is greatly simplified and so is syntax. The most striking examples are the non-use of the copula "be" under some conditions, and then the system of tenses. We can see that either a black speaker says *He live in New York* or a white speaker says *He lives in New York*, the hearer will accept the same message. So in a sense, we can say that Black English is morphprlogically and syntactically less redundant than Standard English.

Variable	Standard English	Black English
Linking verb	He is going.	He – goin'.
Possessive marker	John's cousin	John-cousin
Plural marker	I have five cents.	I got five cent-.
Third-person Singular	He lives in New York.	He live- in New York.
Past tense marker	Yesterday he walked home.	Yesterday he walk- home.

Fig. 6-2 (From Hu Zhuanglin, 1987)

Gender is also an important social factor affecting redundancy. The investigation of gender's effects upon one's linguistic behavior has proved to be a rich resource for examining the correlation of language and society and also one of the main research interests in sociolinguistics. In that area, scholars have done much research on the relationship between gender and language from different aspects such as gender and politeness, gender and language style, gender and miss-communication. Although the study interest is disparate in different research, most of the scholars agree to one point: female is more polite than male; so men speak in a direct way, whose main purpose is transmitting information; while women speak in a relatively indirect and circumlocutory way, whose main purpose is to express feelings and emotions (Yu Guodong, 2002). That is to say, the way of women's expressing gives rise to redundancy. And generally speaking, that marked difference makes women's language more redundant than men. In Lakoff's study (1973), he pointed out eight features in women's language, four of which may bring about redundancy:

(25) Women use more intensifiers and qualifiers, such as *divine*, *charming*, *cute*, *adorable*, etc. Those words were called empty adjectives by

him, which belong to redudancy because they only transmit emotion but contain no information in communication.

(26) Women use more tag questions. Although men and women both tend to use tag questions in some occasions, women even still use them when expressing definite opinions. For instance, "the lecture is wonderful, isn't it?" "The weather is so good, isn't it?"

(27) Women like to use more super polite forms than men such as multiple indirect requesting and their linguistic behavior is more indirect and, hence more polite than men's. For instance, "I was wondering whether it was possible for you to hand me that book ?" And they tend to use more tentative words than men like "I'm afraid that..." "I'm not sure that...", "Maybe I am wrong but...", etc. Those roundabout expressions make their utterances more polite.

(28) Women like to use hypercorrect grammar, whether in grammar rules or phonetics, and they will not use abbreviated forms. For example, they will seldom use "ain't", and they do not say "goin" instead of "going".

All those features in women's language determine that there are more redundancy in their writing or speaking than that of men. The same with cultural factors, we can not say men's language is better than women's just because there are less redundancy, since that is determined by the gender features.

Wardhaugh's research in Thai (1986) also can prove that general rule. In the polite conversation in Thai, women emphasize an action through repeating the same verb several times while men do that just by adding a descriptive verb "mak" after that verb.

本章深入分析了影响冗余度的因素。第一,动机因素在冗余的出现中起着至关重要的作用。正如人类的其他行为一样,语言是思想的外化。我们的大部分语言都是带着某种目的产生和表达的。第二,语境作为另一个因素会影响冗余度。由于我们不重复已经存在于语境中的信息,所以语境对信息具有筛选功能。第三,不同的语言功能会导致不同程度的冗余,正如我们在前一章的例子中所看到的。第四,文体风格。风格越正式,语言就越冗余。此外,还有社会因素,如种族、性别对冗余度都有一定的影响。

Conclusion

The meaning of linguistic redundancy has long been equaled to "wordiness" and "uselessness" in people's daily life. Even some professional linguists regard it as a negative feature of language. However, with a large scale of studies on redundancy from different aspects, people gradually get a relevant objective understanding. The previous research on it can be classified into micro-scopic view and macro-scopic view. The former mainly concerns the redundant elements in linguistic symbol system; while the latter pays attention to redundancy in language use process. We find that lots of cases have not been considered in the latter group, therefore, this book studies redundancy in pragmatics-a macroscopic point of view.

Though pragmatics was once called "the wastebasket" by linguists and philosophers, its explanatory power in some aspects makes it become an important branch of linguistics and a booming period of this discipline has been witnessed in the past decades. Many linguists try to explain different humans communication phenomenan with pragmatics. Accordingly, quite a few influential theories in this field have been put forward. And this book interprets redundancy in terms of some representative theories in pragmatics.

Although some studies have tackled redundancy from the aspect of pragmatic functions, few attempts have been made to interpret it according to pragmatic theories systematically; rhetorical effects of redundancy have been mentioned but there is no detailed analysis, let alone the analysis of it in text. Therefore, this book tries to meet these challenges.

First, in view of the important pragmatic value of redundancy in producing implicature, this book interprets redundancy mainly in terms of three representative pragmatic theories concerning implicature: Cooperative Principle, Relevance Theory and Indirect Speech Acts. We tackle redundancy with three maxims in CP—Quantity maxim, Relation Maxim and maxim of Manner. Redundancy can flout these maxims, which will give rise to conversational implicatures. Relevant Theory views communication as an ostensive-inferential process. Discourse Markers, one kind of redundancy, are ostensive stimuli which can help hearers to choose the most relevant assumptions. And the implicature is the optimal relevance because its contextual effect is the largest while the hearers' effort required to process it is smallest. Circumlocution in redundancy is one of the indirect speech acts, which is expressed in a roundabout way to produce intended implications.

Then, this book analyzes redundancy from the angle of text. Appropriate redundancy in a good text can not only bring about great rhetoric effects—emphasis, expression and description; but also can create a unified and cohesive text. These functions are discussed in Chapter Four in details with the typical data in *Vanity Fair* and William Shakespeare's plays. Through the interpretation and the analysis of the functions, we make a further proof of the value of redundancy in pragmatic field.

Since redundancy is a valuable language phenomenon, there must be some reasons for its existence. Gui Shichun (1980) said: "Without redundancy, language will be nothing more than a withered flower." That is the function of redundancy. In fact, besides the motivation of language users, there are some other factors will result in redundancy such as psychology, style, culture, race and gender, which make redundancy an indispensable feature of language.

In sum, this book discusses redundancy in two aspects: implicature and text. It throws a new light in redundancy and attempts to explore the implicit reasons for its existence.

However, due to limited time, space and material, this book is far from perfect. In order to narrow down the research scope, this book only studies redundancy from two aspects and most of the redundancy data analyzed in this book are from literature works rather than the natural language. That does avoid some interference factors, but the analysis is far from comprehensive to pragmatic studies. Besides that, as an attempt, the exploration of the reasons may be not deep and precise enough. If the follow-up research can make some further discussions and do some special studies on the reasons, it will help us to get a more objective and comprehensive understanding of the nature of this common language phenomenon.

According toVerschueren (2000), using language must consist of the continuous making of linguistic choices, consciously or unconsciously, for language-internal and/or language-external reasons. These choices can be situated at any level of linguistic form: phonetic/phonological, morphological, syntactic, lexical and semantic. They may range over a variety of internal options, or they may involve regionally, socially or functionally distributed types of variation. Moreover, speakers do not only choose forms. They also choose strategies. Choosing a strategy of deference, for example, may require specific choices to be made on a wide range of structural levels, such as language, style, terms of address, lexicon in general, and so on. The most important is that choices are made both in producing and in interpreting an utterance, and both types of choice making are of equal importance for the communication flow and the way in which meaning is generated.

So far we have discussed the definition and nature of redundancy, expounded positive functions of redundancy and analyzed factors that influence the degree of redundancy. The question we have been trying to answer is: what happens to people when using redundancy?

It should be acknowledged that redundancy is just like a coin of two sides. On one hand, too much redundancy is a fault of style; on the other hand, appropriate redundancy can play an important role in language use. So we can say that the use of redundancy is a kind of linguistic choice made by people. Then it is natural to ask why people choose to use redundancy. This is where another important notion, adaptability comes in. "Adaptability is the property of language which enables humans beings to make negotiable linguistic choices from a variable range of possibilities in such a way as to approach points of satisfaction for communicative needs." (Verschueren, 2000). From the previous chapters we can see that redundancy is abundantly used to satisfy both pragmatic and rhetorical needs, so it is the purpose of successful communication that motivates people to employ redundancy.

Another issue of great importance is that we should observe proper degree of redundancy when using it, for properly used redundancy can help us achieve successful communication, while too much of it will become an obstacle. As for how to use it appropriately, we should use redundancy with good measure.

本书结论部分指出:冗余的使用是一种语言选择,甚至是说话者为了他或她的特殊目的而成功交际的一种潜意识选择。我们应该关注冗余的的使用程度。滥用冗余会引起听者的误解甚至厌恶,而恰当地使用冗余是交际的需要,能达到一定的效果,这是我们在语言使用中通过简单或简洁所不能达到的。

Bibliography

英文文献

专著类:

[1] Aitchison, Jean. The Seed of Speech: the Origin and Evolution of Language[M]. Cambridge: Cambridge University Press, 2000.

[2] Austin, J. L. How to do things with words[M]. Beijing: Foreign Language Teaching and Research Press, 2000.

[3] Bahn, Paul G. Ancient Art. In Jones, S., Martin, R. and Pilbeam, D. (eds) The Cambridge Encyclopedia of Human Evolution[M]. Cambridge: Cambridge University Press, 1992.

[4] Blakemore, D. L. Semantic Constraints on Relevance[M]. Oxford: Blackwell. 1987.

[5] Blakemore, D. Understanding Utterance [M]. Oxford: Blackwell. 1992.

[6] Blum - Kulka, House and Kasper (eds.), Norwood. Cross - cultural Pragmatics[M]. NJ: Ablex, 1989.

[7] Bolinger, D. Aspects of language[M]. New York: Harcout Brace Jovanovich, Inc, 1975.